SUCCESS COMES
IN CANS

SUCCESS COMES IN CANS

YOU ARE WHAT YOU SEW

ISAAC ADDAI - DWOMOH

authorHOUSE®

AuthorHouse™
1663 Liberty Drive
Bloomington, IN 47403
www.authorhouse.com
Phone: 1-800-839-8640

Published by AuthorHouse   07/16/2012

ISBN: 978-1-4772-1870-9 (sc)
ISBN: 978-1-4772-1871-6 (hc)
ISBN: 978-1-4772-1872-3 (e)

Contents

Introduction

It is quite interesting to live in this world today not knowing what to do, where to live, where to go, and what the next day has in store for you. How hard it is, not to know where and when the next meal is coming from and the time of its arrival. What about realizing that with a little push you will be able to reach that drop of water to quench your thirst? You would surely understand it better if you had been in any of these situations before.

Remember, this is one area in life that I strongly wish on human being here on earth.

My desire in writing this book is for all to come to their God given potential to overcome the difficulties of this life, so much so that the unexpected could be kept at bay, if not eradicated in totality. There are enough resources on earth for all mankind to live happily. When we come to understand God's love and provisions that have been made available for all mankind, then we will be able to move ahead in this life in order to bring to pass God's vision for all humanity. There is so much we can do to combat the pressure, the hunger, and all the uncertainties of this world. You can only get to your destination if you know where you are going.

You have a part to play, and I also have a part to deal with. Until we all contribute our quota, we will never see the end of human suffering today or tomorrow. We do have all the necessary power, the strength, and the natural resources to make it happen. Your input is so important that it can make difference between life and death. The life we live today is as a result of our actions yesterday. Sow something today, and tomorrow's generation will reap it.

Chapter 1

Life Pursuit

It is always easy to underestimate the achievement of success or prosperity if you are not the very person who made it happen but are just enjoying it. Pursuing success out of nowhere in the world today is one of the most difficult ventures. It is somehow easy to make it when the family you were born into has already made it, but to come from nowhere takes faith, determination, persistence, hard work, sacrifice, focus, and the grace of God.

For success to come my way, I have to believe first and foremost that I am capable of making it to my destination and that I am a winner. I need to desire success more than anything. This is what will set me up to pursue in the things I want out of this life. I should be determined to win and not fail, get to my destination and not drop out, cross the finished line and not give up. Yes there will be setbacks. I will rise and fall. There will be mountains and valleys. Situations may be unbearable at times, and things may not go the way I expected. The mountains may be too steep to climb and valleys too deep to overcome, but there is one thing that matters—if I fall and my mouth is wallowing in the mud, there is only one thing that matters, I will arise, shake myself off and continue. I will have to persist until my desire comes to pass. There would be areas of my life that I may need to adjust and sacrifices may also need to be made in order for the vision to come to pass. With constant focus and the grace of God the dreams would come to pass.

Only a few people know my beginning and where I come from. One word to describe myself would be 'nobody'. And, to be honest with you, that was in the eyes of men. You are nobody when your mother, father, brother, sisters, uncles, and aunties have not made it from my kind of world. When it comes to success and prosperity these words was nowhere to be found in my family. I am not comparing success to prosperity in what the world will describe or refer to in the sense of millionaires, business men and women, entrepreneurs, and famous people. I am only referring to success and prosperity as having enough to eat, drink, and wear on a given day; enough for everyone in the family and those in need in any given occasion or situation.

I am the ninth born in my family from my maternal side but in terms of my father's offspring, I am the seventeenth child out of twenty-three. Just imagine what that family looked like in any given situation. Any average father or mother would understand the situation and stress associated with it—not only for the parent but also for the children. There was never enough at any given time for everyone in the family, not to mention outsiders.

Everyday basic amenities were always scarce, and there was never enough food for everyone.

Adequate clothing was also missing. It was only once a year that the boys would receive two yards of java print and four yards for the girls. For the boys the material would be sown into a shirt and shorts. For the girls it was a skirt and a blouses. This would only happen when the cocoa harvest was good. Just imagine having this piece of clothing wrapped around your body for a whole year. After few months the colours faded and sometimes tore apart with holes. It was sometimes impossible to keep these clothes on your body. In case something happened to your clothes, you had to walk around naked for the rest of the year. If you wear rags, you do not wrestle.

Having slippers or sandals was also deemed a luxury. I never remember wearing them during my early years. In such a family, one needs to be very careful, for whatever you do would have a great impact on the family. You have no choice as to what to eat or drink because you have to do with whatever is set before you. As the proverbs goes 'a beggar has no choice'.

I am writing this in tears today and asking myself why was I subjected to such a lifestyle that wasn't my fault. What went wrong? What could my parents have done better? I often ask myself if my parents could see the circumstances they subjected us to.

I started school at the age of six instead of five, something which is still mystery to me. Was it because my father was not able to pay the fees in order for me to start? Or there were others who have to start before me but were waiting their turn.

I had only one set of school uniforms, which I considered lucky. It was an obligation imposed on every parent to make sure a child had uniform before they came to school. I had to wear the same uniform five times in a week, Monday to Friday, and then I had to wash it on Saturdays. If something was to have happened to it, that would have been the end of my school life, because there would be no replacement. I remember having holes in my school uniform sometimes.

Because of financial strains, most of my brothers and sisters dropped out of school at a very young age to help on the farm. We who were left in school struggled not to mention those who were handicapped in terms of learning. When it came to books and pens, I had to borrow from friends. I had to do tricks to secure me access to use other people materials. I needed to help others who were struggling with their school work as compensation for what they lend me.

I managed to secure a move from the country to the city with my brother who had a small business in a busy centre. I was to earn my mat space by making sure I was always amongst the first four in class when my school report came or else I would have to move back to the country.

City life for me at the age of ten was not a luxury. I had earned it through working very hard. Every day after school, I had to go to my brother's wife's shop to help out selling ice water. I had to work from 3 p.m. to 10 p.m. before I could go home to prepare for the next school day.

To be honest, I really lost my childhood. There were no friends, no games, no outings, and no one to look up to. I had to take each day as it came. I was surviving instead of living. I realized that life was depreciating each day; therefore, it was necessary to work things out to my favour. Whilst helping out at the shop I decided to have a sweet table selling sweets and biscuits in front of the kiosk. This sweet table became a rich source of income, helping to buy my school materials and basic necessities.

At the age of twelve, I passed my common entrance exams as I was not able to do it at the age of eleven due to lack of money. It was one thing to pass and another to be able to go to the next level of school since it was impossible for poor children.

My mum and dad could not afford it, but I had passed with a half scholarship in one of the best schools in the country. Who was going to pay the rest? My brother at that time was struggling equally, but it would have been a disgrace if nothing was done to help me. He therefore decided to pay the fees. Although it was not much, it was very difficult to pay.

Having passed the exams, I needed to go for an interview. But who was to take me there? No one made himself or herself available. This is one particular experience I will never forget in my life. I had to travel one 120 miles to the school for the interview on my own. This was at the age of twelve. Today, one of my boys is twelve years and I have to pick him from school every day. In those days, no one bothered and no one cared whether I went or not.

I didn't even know how to get there, but I made some enquiries. To be honest, I made that journey in tears. Unable to get a bus straight to the school, I had to make a connection in a nearby town. It was late in the night, so I missed my connecting bus and became stranded at the bus stop. I knew no one at that town and had no extra money except my return bus fare. The only thing I could do was stay at the bus station until the next morning. It was late at night when a woman I had never met before realized my situation and took me home to stay for the night. I never saw this woman again. It is my prayer that God will richly bless and keep her. She was God sent. It always makes me realize that in time of need God always make provisions abound for his children.

I was successful with the interview and gained admission to the school. It was at this school that I spent five years of my youthful life. None of my parents or any member of my family ever visited me in my school. I was more or less an orphan, just passing through life with no one. Whilst other students were receiving visitors at the end of every week, I had no one to visit me. The suffering, the fears, and the pains were unbearable—no friends, no parents, and no relatives. For me, it was either make it or break. It was either I persevered with the education or go back to my family's home.

To be honest, I felt that there was no point in going on, but my inner intuition compelled me to continue. I had to convince myself that there was something in there for me. My future would depend on it. We are destroyed for lack of knowledge, so it was necessary to have that education. If you give someone bread, it will only be sufficient for a few weeks, but if you educate a child, you sustain him for life. Life was unbearable, but I needed to continue.

When it was time to come home for holidays at the end of a term, I had to borrow money from fellow students or one of the masters to pay my lorry fare. At home, I was always given a one-way ticket back to school with a promise of more money later, but it never arrived. Why? What did I do wrong? Did I deserve to be punished for going to school? Was it my fault that my parents were poor? Why did the basic necessities of life become a big issue?

Even basic textbooks were a big problem. I had to copy from other student's textbooks to be able to cope with the academic requirements. Anytime I ordered anything from school outside my school fees I was made to work during holidays to pay for it or be punished. Ordering even normal exercise books, pens, and pencils was impossible for me, even though I was given half scholarship by the school.

My entire school days were sad times for me as a student. There was never a day I enjoyed school, because I lacked the basic necessities that make a student. Don't forget what I had to go through at the hands of other students who were only there because their parents had so much money and were unable to control their children at home.

It was just after my secondary education that I really understood the proverb 'life is how you make it'. I decided to do something with my life. The brother I was staying with travelled when I was in the third year of secondary school. I had to go and live in my uncle's house but not to depend upon him. There was no support from there either. I had to fend for myself both food and clothing. At least I had a roof to cover my head.

After my final exams, I went home and decided to find myself a job. Life was like being tossed into the sea in the middle of nowhere, and I had to survive. It was either I swim to survive or sink and die. Luckily, I was not paying rent, which was the only good thing about my situation, but I needed to feed and clothe myself. I washed my shirt overnight in order to be able to wear it the following day. This life compelled me to look at my circumstances to see how I could change it.

I had no proper qualification and was still young, so, jobs were hard to find. I had to find something that will bring in money or else join my parents on the farm. That would be a U-turn. I decided therefore to sell bread and egg sandwiches in front of a nearby hotel. This was a place where travellers come in from different cities and towns to rest for the night. Those who cannot afford the hotel food would come out and buy from the petty traders on the roadside. This was the beginning of my breakthrough. It was not an easy task. I had to make sure all the products were ready during the day, and between 6 p.m. and 2 a.m., I had to do the selling. I prepared the omelettes and the sandwiches to the best of my knowledge in order to keep the customers coming. The price I charged was very competitive though the profit margin was very small. But I did better than break even due to the large quantities I sold. With the income from the business I was able to register at a school to do my advanced-level certificate. It was at this school that I studied accounting, economics, and government.

After the two years, I applied for a teaching position at a nearby international school. It was within a walking distance. The money that came in was good but not enough compared to the proceeds that came from the sandwich business. However, I was not discouraged because it was a more decent job.

If you want to get somewhere, you need to rise up and go. Never try to skip a gradient and never give up.

I had to find something, because I needed more money. Having discussed it with the principal of the school, I managed to find a business man who was looking for a private teacher for his children in the evening. This was a turning point in my life. I was able to save some money and to afford decent meals and some clothes.

It was at this time that I managed to get a passport done, which in those days cost an arm and a leg. It was something which only the rich were able to acquire, so this was a big breakthrough. It didn't come on a silver platter. I had to work very hard for it, working at odd and ungodly hours. Remember, success comes with sacrifice.

I had no friends or colleagues to socialize with. I kept to myself. I realized the road ahead would be rough. I had no backstop, virtually no one to catch me if I fell, but I was determined to make it in life. Life is sometimes like a roller coaster, ups and downs. For me the downs were more than the ups, and I needed to make sure I come out of that uncomfortable zone. It was an uphill struggle coming from nowhere. But I was determined. I had acidulous character and was not ready to take no for an answer.

I came from a place where you said your father's name and people simply recognized you, but that was not true in my case. The moment I called my father's name he was mistaken for someone else, all because he was not able to make a name for himself during his lifetime. May he rest in perfect peace?

If you are that man or woman who wants to make it in life, someone who wants to get somewhere, prosper and become successful in life, then remember you have to work for it. Your vision and dreams will come to pass with much business. Yes, some may have a head start and for some, success will be handed to them on a silver platter. But if you're like me, you may have to pull against all the odds against you to make it happen. One thing I will always advise is that no matter how success is handed down to you, you need to maintain it and work at it in order to grow and to increase. I always have a saying that if you're handed a room full of money and you do not work with it, it will one day be gone. This is the more reason why the sea is always waiting for its share of the rain.

Having received my passport, I started traveling and importing goods from the West African countries on a very small scale, having managed to secure myself a mini shop at the city centre. I was able to save enough money from the business to further my education. In the back of my mind I knew knowledge was essential in a man's life. Just as the Bible says for lack of knowledge my people perish. I did not want to perish but to gain knowledge and understanding. I started working on it.

In 1985, I had a three years scholarship to study in England. This was the most important breakthrough in my life. Where there is a will there is always a way. Desiring to pursue my education I accepted the invitation to travel to England. On arrival, before I was able to do my degree in business management, I had to study scientology and dienectics, which was contrary to my belief system. I spent only five weeks at the college and then moved to London where I enrolled in a business college. All was not well until I enrolled in a Bible college where I studied for four years. The rest is history.

Now I have a family and we are able to afford to eat three square meals a day, to buy what we need, and to travel where we like. Remember where I started from, and you will realize that the good Lord have been on my side. He has surely destined me for bigger things. I haven't laid my tools down yet. I am even working harder than I when I started. There is one thing I know—the end shall be good. Now there is no mountain too high to climb, no rivers too big to cross, no tunnel too long, too low, or too smelly to crawl through. I always know the end shall be good. The hills and valleys may come my way; the wind and storm will arise; the smoke and darkness of this life may come also. And if all things become like shadows in this life, there is one thing I know: that I can make it. My end shall be bigger than my beginning. I don't allow myself to be bugged down by circumstances.

Yes, life is full of ups and downs, but I always make sure that there are fewer downs. Try as much as possible in this life to avoid unnecessary causalities if you can. I believe that you can—big or small, high or low, visible or invisible, in the dark or in the light, in the day or in the night, hot or cold, and dry or wet. With God on your side all things are possible. He is no respecter of persons. Have the will and there will be a way.

Chapter 2

God Given Powers

I have been very upset over the years in hearing people putting limits on themselves. They say things such as: I can't go there; I can't do that; this is not for me; I am not up to that; this is not within my ability; leave that to the experts; and many more. If you are going to get somewhere in this life you have to rise and go for it. Set our heart and mind on things higher than you to achieve them. It is when you say that you can't, that you fail. Winners are those who say to themselves they can and rise to the challenge. You will never know success or failure until you arise and act. You need to make use of your God given power that was invested in you during creation.

We cannot sit down here and talk about success and prosperity without looking at the Genesis account of the Scriptures about what God created man to be. How were we created? Was it to be prosperous? Or to be stricken with poverty, living our lives in deprivation and disappointments? Is it in an uncalled for destitution or in abundance? What does life have in store for you? Why live if there is nothing good in store for you? What kind of life did God intend for his creatures when He made them? Did God bless them or cursed them? Were some men created to be more equal than others?

These are but few of the many questions that we tend to ask when things do not go the way we want. Because of our lack of understanding in God's creation we tend to blame God sometimes.

We even question why we were made the colour we have. If white, we think we are superior and, if black, we think we are cursed. We even use our colour to blame ourselves for the predicaments that come our way. We tend to brand ourselves as failures in the things that we have not even started. We blame our parents, our teachers, our bosses, our spouses, our friends, and even our society and the community we live in for our failures and our low self-esteem. Yes, there are some societies that will treat you as a dog or a nobody, but that does not change who you are in the sight of God or what God has made you to be. If we know our status in the sight of God, no amount of degradation in the society that we live in will matter. It will not matter how people will put you down.

Arise and take your God given place on the world stage where you live. We should never think that some people are more human than others. Why do we sometime have an inferiority complex if all men were created in the image of God and if God has a purpose for each one of us? It is about time we go to the drawing board to check our maker's master plan for all mankind. This will reveal the truth of our lives. For, if we know the truth, it will set us free.

With just a quick look at the book of Genesis we will come to the place of understanding our place here on earth.

Genesis 1: 26-28:

> Then God said "let us make man in our image,
> in our likeness, and let them rule over the fish of
> the sea and the birds of the air, over the livestock,
> over all the earth, and over all the creatures that
> move along the ground." So God created man in
> his own image, in the image of God he created
> him male and female he created them. God
> blessed them and said to them, be fruitful and
> increase in number fill the earth and subdue it.
> Rule over the fish of the sea and the birds of the
> air and over every living creature that moves on
> the ground.

From these Scriptures, the first thing that believers should discover about themselves is that we were created in the image and the likeness of God. We were made in a special manner by our God. Due to our place of importance in God's agenda we were the last thing that God created. God made sure all the things necessary for man's comfort and survival are all in place before embarking on a journey to make us.

The Scriptures make it clear that all other things created were only called into being, but when it came to man, God took his time to make us. This alone was an indication of how special we were in the sight of God. It was a great honour and favour of God, our creator, toward mankind. Man, as soon as he was made, had everything necessary for his comfort at his fingertips. The creation of man was more signal and an immediate act of divine wisdom and power than that of the other creatures. God took special time in making what He would cherish and have good relationship with. It pleased God to make man in his own express image, calling a council together to consider of the making of man.

In seeing Christ Jesus, we need to realize that God made us nothing less than himself. We have God's image and his likeness. Christ is the very express image of God's person as the son of the father, the only begotten.

It was both male and female that God created with no difference or limitation for any of them. It was also both that God blessed, not cursing any of them as seems the case in some societies. God made both to increase and also to multiply. It is when men takes up their place in the plan of God can we replenish the earth—a duty bestowed upon man only not any other thing that God created. To accomplish and fulfil God's plan and purpose of replenishing the earth man was blessed and given the ability to be fruitful and multiply. The pronouncing of a blessing upon man was a virtue of which their posterity should extend to the utmost corners of the earth and continue to the utmost period of time.

The other greatest weapon that God gave unto man was authority and dominion over all the things he created. Even though man does not provide for any of them, he has power over every living thing on the face of the earth. Authority was given to man to overcome the entire world in which he has been created in. All these gifts were imputed to man's life for his benefit.

Galatians 3: 8 also indicates that God preached the gospel to our father Abraham. The good news preached to him was about the blessing of God in his life. Come to think of it, we will realize that the gospel is all about blessing. If it is a blessing, why do some of us live as though we have been cursed? God intended his created beings to enjoy the best of this life. God's world was meant to be trouble free, poverty free, famine free, and sickness free. It seems the word of our own mouth and also our sins have reduced us to nothing, reducing our blessings, our power, and our dominion that was given to us. It has eroded them away before our very eyes. It is about time we come back to base and realize where we have fallen short of God's grace and favour. We need to get right with God, our maker, in order to enjoy the benefits given to us at the very beginning.

When you fall on your face in the mud and you remain there, wet and dripping with mud, cold, shaking, there will be no hope for you. Instead, if you arise, shake the dust and mud off your face, and move in the right direction, you will surely get to your destination. The end is always within reach if we are determined. The victory belongs to us if we don't quit or give up but confront situation squarely.

Abraham, having received the good news preached to him, did not consider his own body dead according to his age of 100 years, nor did he acknowledge deadness of his wife Sarah's womb. The Scripture says that he did not staggered at the promise of God through unbelief, but he was strong in faith, giving glory to God. Abraham was fully persuaded that he that had promise was able to perform. What God promised, he has the power and ability to perform. He didn't go back on his promise, and neither is he a man that he should lie.

We must grow to trust in God our maker. The promises of God are "yes," but the "Amen" is by us. He does not override our will. When we yield to him, he will direct us. He is faithful, and that has been promised. Man is unique and blessed. We can increase, multiply, and also become fruitful. We have God given authority and power to go forth and achieve victory and success in all the areas of our life in this world today.

I know many Christians are waiting to get to heaven before they enjoy the blessing of God their creator. I strongly believe the Bible teaches more than that. We are to enjoy the blessing of God here and now on this very earth. God has given us all the resources, the ability, the power, the strength, and the wisdom to tap into all the resources that He has placed on the earth. If they are not necessary, why create them? When God created the heavens and the earth and all that there is, he realized that these were all good for man that He had created. As believers, the good of the land belong to us. We need to come to the fullness of God and tap into his resources for ourselves and also for our families.

I strongly believe that many will weep and lament when the Lord Jesus appear in his glory. This will not be because of his presence but because these men and women refused to take what could have been theirs whilst they were on earth. The earth resources are our inheritance. Remember, these would not come to you unless you and I commanded them to come. No one can do away with your God given inheritance but you. Learn to keep your God given blessings and authority, and success will be yours.

Chapter 3

Who Am I?

My destiny depends on the realization of who I am. This knowledge will bring me to the place where I am supposed to be and where I can go. The world and the things in it are so much that there would always be enough for every one of us, so long as we know who we are and what we want. There is no limit to what one can achieve under the sun. The sky should always be your limit, but success comes in "cans" and not in "can'ts".

The knowledge of your ability, your resources, your chances, your strength, and your desire to succeed will always bring you to your destination. Remember, you are somebody that is born under the sun, and you also live under the sun. You therefore have every right to the things under the sun. Since you belong here, you have the right to the things of this world. There should therefore be no limitation to the things that you can or want to achieve. Nothing comes to you by chance unless you take it or fight for it. Nothing comes to you by chance unless you work for it and you desire to have it. What belongs to you will only come if you take it.

Those who think all things are under the control of the Devil should also bear in mind that it was first given to man before we handed it over to the Devil or Satan. If we want it, we can take it back. This is where the problem is. You and I were born in the image of God and have the authority to this world and it's asserts. Legally, they belong to us, and we can always fight for it through the right channel. This channel is through the finished work of Jesus Christ. He is the one who brought back the very thing we lost in the garden to the Devil.

One in a million

I am unique, so are you. I am a winner and a survivor. There is no one like me. I was selected out of a million before I was even conceived in the womb. All those who struggled with me were brought to nothing. They couldn't make it, but I made it. There were so many instances that I was to lose my position and my survival but to no avail.

At the right time and at the right place, I was conceived, even though there were so many spermatogenesis cells that were released. I was the only sperm nucleus that was selected and chosen to enter the egg-cell membrane to fertilize it. For nine months, being an embryo and then a fetus supported by the placenta in the uterus I became a survivor. I was then released to take my place in the unknown world. I was held aloft and placed on a pinnacle with no challenger left.

I am absolutely sure that this was the design of God, my maker—to place me in a winning and blessed world he had ordained for me. I took my place of victory. I was a winner at the time of conception, so how much more now that I am alive and kicking? He that separated me from my mother's womb is capable enough to separate me from poverty. If it pleased God to separate me from my mother's womb against all odds, then all men should be aware that I am a winner. I do not count myself out; I always count myself in. I am surely born victorious, and no one takes that from me. Winning and success are my destiny, and I have settled for that and nothing less. I may not experience it now but at the right time and at the right place it will happen. I am one in a million, and that settles it.

Born to prosper

The man who prospers in life is the one who believes in himself and that he can make it. His faith brings him to the level where he is challenged, compelled, and determined to succeed. This man can accept all the situations that come his way but does not allowed them to deter him. Instead, he uses these situations to work to his advantage. He stays focused, not double minded, and never gives up or quits. He runs his race with perseverance, consistency, endurance, and determination. He operates in the level of faith that he has developed. This person is fully persuaded that he who created him is capable enough to bring him to the level that he has ordained for him.

He always has the knowledge that no matter what happens on his way, his end shall be good. How well do you know yourself? Are you someone with inferiority complex, saying to yourself that you can't make it? Who are you anyway? Until you know who you are, your true self would never be known. Your potential will always be determined by your identity.

When Paul identified himself with the Lord Jesus Christ, he saw the glory of God in his life. He said he had been crucified with Christ, and he no longer lives but Christ lives. This is where Paul found his boldness to be the Paul we have come to know. He that finds his identity is one who does not allow himself to be afraid or to be intimidated, because he or she no longer lives but lives in Christ. It was this that compelled him to say I can do all things through Christ that strengthens me. If Christ is capable, then I, Paul, am also capable. Paul's focus was not on himself but on Jesus who he had believed. You are no different. For it is only in Christ that you can do all things with no limitation.

We need to understand that it is God's will that we prosper. He wants us to prosper in body, spirit, and soul. Since there are not only a selected few who have been promised prosperity, why do you count yourself out of his promises? You need to count yourself in when it comes to the things of God. Your choice will make the difference between success and failure. Remember your success is in your own hands. If I have God given potential, then what stops me from receiving the things of God? If I am in the perfect will of God, then I need to take the things of the kingdom. If the promises of God are yes and perfect, then I just need to say "Amen" to them.

Are you one of those who do not want to try because of the fear of failure?

Remember, 90 per cent of the most successful men and women we see around us started their lives and businesses with difficulties and even failures, but they did not quit because of that. They hung in there and victory became theirs. These are the people who believed in themselves that the end shall be good even though it may terry. Jesus is the one who said his grace is sufficient for us and his strength is made perfect in our weakness. We are sometimes like the young antelope who danced herself lame before the main dance was yet to come. We want to walk before finding our feet. Don't forget the moment you skip a gradient you will fall flat on your face.

But he who falls and rises from his grave will surely avoid the next fall that comes his way. If we know who we are, then we can rest assured that God has a plan and a purpose for our lives. Remember it is a plan for you to prosper and to give you an expected end.

Prosperity is defined as the ability to use God's power to work on our behalf or to meet man's needs. David grew very prosperous but then in *Psalms 23: 1, he cried that "the Lord is my shepherd I shall not want"*. When you know who you are and whose son you belong to, there is no need to be intimidated. If God is your shepherd then your supply is everlasting.

Prosperity is also receiving from God the terms of the covenant blessing. If your blessing is not materializing, then you need to ask yourself if you are in covenant with God. Prosperity is a by-product of our salvation, which comes down to us from the Lord of glory. The book of Galatians makes it plain that through Christ the blessing of Abraham and the promise of the Spirit is received by the Gentiles in faith. Our covenant with the Lord Jesus opens the door to our prosperity and then success.

In the book of James we read that every good and perfect gift is from above and it comes down from the father of light. Jesus is the father of light. If we have been redeemed by Him, then our prosperity, which is a good gift and perfect as well, will be delivered by Him. It is our covenant right to be blessed. When Abraham had a covenant with God he was promised blessing and was truly blessed. He also promised to bless Isaac and Jacob and he surely did. You and I are no different. Remember, God is capable to bringing to pass all the promises he has given us.

Solomon declared that it is the Lord's power that gives wealth. This was true in his father David's life as well as in his, and we are no different. So also did Moses declare that it is God's power that gives us wealth. It is not by our hard work to boast of, but it is his will to all men and women who believe in him and take him at his word. Since we are in Christ, prosperity is necessary to establish our covenant with God.

Success and prosperity are a believer's covenant directly from our covenant partner. We need to let his promise in Mark 11: 24 work in our life. It says, "whatsoever thing you ask when you pray believe that you receive them and you shall have them". This is one of the areas in most people's lives where they get it wrong. They pray and therefore think that is enough. Others also believe that God can do it and therefore never open their mouths to ask. Some also have the desire and pray but do not have the courage to receive what God has promised them. They always put God in a box and try to manipulate the will of God for their lives. We should remember that our God supplies our needs and not our wants. When we allow the four principles listed in the above verse to operate in our life then the mountain would move. The more of the word of God is in us, the more we will understand the principles of faith for success in our lives as believers. If I have the word and pray, then I can have my desire.

Success comes in cans and not in can'ts

The question is, do you have the desire to be successful? Over the years, I have come across many people from many different background and cultures, but then I realized that the above principle works for each one of them. Yes, it works irrespective of colour, gender, or race. Both those who said they can and those who say they can't are all right. People who say they can always have their minds set to make it irrespective of what comes their way.

These people always believe in themselves that they can

a) They believe in themselves that they are winners.

b) They think and plan to succeed.

c) They pursue their goals and implement what they set out to do.

d) Where necessary, they seek advice and ask for help.

e) They never give up, even when they fail at the first try.

f) They put their faith to work and never allow situations to intimidate them.

What about those who say they can't

a) They have no self-confidence in themselves.

b) They are easily intimidated.

c) Because of their mindset, they never sit down to think or plan.

d) They have no goal or plan of their own; they tend to forget that, if you don't know where you are going, any road would lead you there.

e) Even when they try, they quit at the first hurdle, and they fall flat on their faces.

f) They allow fear to derail them from their vision.

I am always sad for people who rule themselves out of any challenge that comes their way. They simply can't see what lies behind the hurdle and get over it. Any hill they see becomes a mountain that is impossible to climb. Any stream they come across becomes a sea impossible to cross. Washed with their inferiority complex, they are filled with I can't do this and I can't do that, I can't go there and I am not trained in that, and I can't join them and all the different can'ts you can think of. We need to remember that we are given the brain to think, so let us think and not allow anyone put an impediment or limitation on us. It is only you who can disqualify yourself. Always have the right mindset and success will be yours. You know where you want to go and what you want to do and know that the best belongs to you. One needs to work and strive for it. Success doesn't come by chance. Yes, failure may come at times, but those who fall and rise up again and shake off the dust, press on the mark are those that succeed and make it in life. Truly, success comes in cans and not in can't.

Abraham's blessings

What can we learn from Abraham's blessing? Genesis 28: 3-4 says, "May God Almighty bless you and make you fruitful and multiply you, that you may be an assembly of people; and give you the blessing of Abraham, to you and your descendants with you, that you may inherit the land in which you are a stranger, which God gave to Abraham".

We often hear people sing that the blessing of Abraham belongs to them. What is it to us? We know we were redeemed from the curse of the law that the blessing of Abraham may be imputed upon us. Who are those who are the children of Abraham? It is those who walk and live in faith. These are the descendants of Abraham. Not necessarily the twelve tribes of Israel. Remember, it was when Abraham believed in God that it was imputed to him for righteousness. So, when we believe, the blessings of Abraham would also be ours.

Come to think of it, we believers need to understand the gospel that was preached to Abraham our father. It was no other gospel than the good news of blessing. There is no other gospel to us today than the same gospel which was given to Abraham.

Those who are of faith are the children of Abraham, and the blessing of Abraham belongs to them. We don't necessary have to pray for a blessing, it belongs to us. Paul put it in a very nice way in Galatians 3: 13-14: "Christ has redeemed us from the curse of the Law having become a curse for us (for it is written curse is everyone who hangs on a tree) that the blessings of Abraham might come upon us the Gentile in Christ Jesus that we might receive the promise of the Spirit through faith".

The prince does not necessary go round, asking people to make him a prince. Since he is the son of the king, he is a prince automatically. The title will remain even if the king, his father dies. He is an heir to the throne. All the subjects of the kingdom do not contest against him. It is only when you are not aware of who you are that the Devil and others contest with you for your position. When something belongs to you, you don't go about asking for it to be given to you. You just take it.

In faith, the blessing of Abraham belongs to us. There is no need to fight for what belongs to you. Our faith in God is the guarantee of our blessing. When you and I seek first the kingdom and his righteousness, all others shall be added to us. Those who see the blessing of God in their lives are those who realize that the blessing of Abraham belongs to them. Their lives and speech are a testimony to that fact. It is not something they fight for or struggle to attain, it is their God given gift, and no one can take it away from them.

Remember, your faith level will determine the level of what you receive and the level of your success. The earth's resources belong to the believer, but how many of us tap into them and appreciate them? Most Christians live like beggars. Don't you know that we have been made both priests and kings? As kings, all things of the kingdom belong to us. Just take a step back and look at the godly kings of Israel and Judah and how prosperous and successful they were when they walked in obedience to the word of God. A closer look at King David and King Solomon reveals how fulfilled they were in the sight of God who called and made them kings over his people. Neither did the priest in the biblical days suffer any lack. At least they were entitled to 10 per cent of whatever any citizen earned or were blessed with. Our blessings as children of God are bestowed upon us due to the finished work of our Lord and Saviour Jesus Christ.

Our father Isaac was in covenant with God and was also covered by the blessings of Abraham, meaning the blessings of his father were also bestowed upon him. In obedience to the word of God that came to him he saw the blessings of God in his life.

One may wonder why I am talking about obedience. It is the only element that brings us to the level where we apply the blessings of God in our life. Through the prophet Isaiah the Lord spoke to the people of Israel that if they are willing and obedient they would eat the good of the land but if they rebel they would be devoured with the sword. The good of the land promised in the book of Isaiah does not come to most Christians because they are not willing and obedient.

When Isaac was eight days old he was circumcised. As a boy, he was separated from his brother Ishmael when his father received explicit direction from God to cast out the bond woman and her child. This act deprived Isaac of a brother's love, but when God instructed him to remain in Gerar and not go to Egypt he obeyed. He was to remain in the land, which the Lord had promised to give the descendants of Abraham as inheritance. It was the place where the blessing of God could overflow.

Isaac went to the Philistine city of Gerar, and there, fearing for his life, he passed off his wife as his sister—an act that his father had done before him. He was justly rebuked by Abimelech the king for his duplicity. Isaac then pitched his camp in the valley of Gerar and became prosperous as a wheat grower and a herdsman. Due to this, the envious Philistines began a systematic, petty harassment by stopping the wells that his father, Abraham, had dug. He was advised to leave Gerar in the interest of peace. Subsequently, Isaac returned to Beersheba upon Abimelech advice. There the Lord appeared unto him at night and promised to bless him for his father Abraham's sake.

Christians are equally blessed because of the blessings of Abraham that are bestowed upon us. We always need to remind ourselves that these blessings come by faith in the Lord Jesus Christ. Isaac had to walk the direction that God gave him. It is when we come to reason with the Lord God in faith that we receive our God given blessings.

Yes, you are a man that God has created to achieve. Are you one who has the power to get wealth? One who need not be intimidated by the Devil or any other person? One in whom faith has to arise within to take the things of the kingdom? That is who you are.

Chapter 4

The Power of Sowing and Reaping

Just as the natural law of sowing and reaping works, so also does the spiritual law. There is no boundary or hindrance to this law of sowing and reaping. It works for a child, and it also works for the old. It works for the blacks, and so also does it work for the white—for the male and also for the female. Whatever you sow will produce after its kind. If you plant apples you will reap apples. If you sow avocados you will surely reap avocados. This law cannot be changed. If you want potatoes and you sow tomato seeds, it will not work. There is no way you can change the end product from what was sown at the beginning. Even though your sowing method can change and the quantity and quality can also change, the seed that was sown will always be the same as the one that is harvested. What you sow is what you will surely reap.

My Dad was a cocoa farmer and a very good one, too. He really knew how to get the good seed at harvest time. His farming methods also helped him to increase the yield needed at the end of the farming season. During his time of farming, the cocoa seeding took seven years to produce after its kind, and it continued to yield through the subsequent years. There was never a time that the cocoa beans turned into coffee beans. There was no amount of weeding, pruning, or pest controlling that was able to influence the seed that was sown. Though the quality and the quantity may have changed, the seed never changed. The seed sown will always be similar to the one that we reap.

It is equally true with the spiritual law of sowing and reaping. If I sow love, I will reap love. If I sow hatred, I will also reap hatred. If I give, it shall be given back to me. The only difference in my sowing whether in love, hatred, or giving would be the increase that will take place, confirming the principle of the law. The more, therefore, that I give, the more that I will receive. The more I love, the more I will be loved.

The Kingdom principles

Mark 4: 26 helps us to understand this principle very well. It reads "And he said the Kingdom of God as if a man should cast seed into the ground". This indicates to us that the spiritual law of sowing and reaping is equal to the natural law of sowing and reaping. The sower sows the seed, leaves it, and it goes to sleep. How it springs up, no one knows. The growth comes not from the sower's efforts but from God's given power bestowed upon the seed. It is what is known as the natural law as ordained by God the creator. The Genesis accounts indicate that this law will never cease or change. There will always be seedtime and harvest. If it is unchangeable natural law ordained by God, what then prevents me from allowing this law to work or operate in my life situation? Why can't it work to my favour?

If I am determined and sow the seed of success in my life, then I will surely be successful. The seed that I sow will determine the harvest that I shall reap. My seed at the time of harvest is the produce of what I sow in spring. During the summer months, because I desired to have some organic vegetables at home, I decided to sow some seeds in my garden. Then came autumn when I visited the crops, I realized that the plants were full of vegetables. Tomatoes, peppers, beans, and peas were all harvested but from different plants in the garden.

My success today is as a result of my sowing yesterday. It will be good if I did sow good seed to receive good harvest. The law of sowing and reaping works both in my body and in my finances as well. It works with the physical seeds that I put on the ground as well as the words that proceed out of my mouth. They both yield their fruit in their seasons. This principle works both in the physical as well as spiritual realm.

In the Kingdom of Heaven the word is what the sower sows. The very principle that helps a seed to germinate and bear fruit, giving bread to the eater and seed to the sower equally, works in the words that we speak. If the word that I speak is as a seed, then whatever I say will germinate as a seed and bear fruit to bless me. This, therefore, needs to bring me to a place where I realize that whatever I say has an effect on my life, whether for good or for evil. My seed is in my words. My blessings or cursing are in my own mouth. If I am able to control my words, then I can control my life. If we are in the Kingdom then we should live by the Kingdom's principles.

This principle helps one to understand why some are in good shape when it comes to business and others are not. It shows why some live luxuriously and others live in poverty. It indicates why some have money in abundance but others find it difficult to earn a square meal in a given day. Our future is really shaped by the words of our mouth today. I know of a woman who had no formal education who became very prominent in her society due to the words of her mouth. The words we speak would always set us on high or bring us down. Our words are our spiritual force, which works for us or against us depending on what we are saying or what we have said in the past.

The principles of sowing and reaping are very simple. The words are the seed that we sow; the heart is the ground on which the seeds are sown; the lips or the mouth (or a pen of a writer) are like the hands that we use to sow the seeds. What we sow in the heart would equally bear fruit as what is sown on the ground. It is what is in the heart that the mouth will speak because the harvest has come. One can never speak what is not on the heart. If you have a small vocabulary, you can only speak a few words like a child who is learning how to talk. It is only the words that he or she is taught that he or she is able to speak back when asked. It is what is generated in the heart that the mouth will speak. It is what is spoken out of the heart that the spiritual force backs to bring to pass.

Believers should bear it in mind that the Devil only comes against us for one thing, and that is our faith. The word of God in your heart is powerful and able to destroy the works of the enemy or the Devil when spoken. When the Devil is able to destroy our faith, he would always win victory over us. There is no victory outside our faith. Faith in your own words and faith in oneself makes the difference between life and death, between success and failure, between first and last, between the rich and the poor, between light and darkness, between the head and the tail. Have faith in yourself and faith in the word of God. In whatever business you find yourself, be positive about it. Believe that it will work, it will prosper, and it will increase and multiply. Remember negative confession and attitude will always spread like cancer to destroy the very thing we plan to do. It will spread through your own words or through your own partners to harm and then destroy you.

Acting on what you believe

One thing I always advise people is to do the things they believe in. There are so many examples in the Bible with regard to men and women who were able to receive their miracles through their faith. What they confessed serve as the avenue through which they saw the blessings of God in their lives. Though some of the situations they went through were impossible in the eyes of men, God honoured their words and delivered them

David and Goliath (1 Samuel 17: 31-49)

David was not different from the normal descendants of Abraham but was able to choose his words carefully because he realized the power of words. He realized that words were like seeds that are sown. He had faith in the word of God that what He had promised he would be able to perform. David was just a young man who was attending to his father's business, tending the sheep of the family. Jesse, his father, asked him to take to his brothers; ephah; parched corn, and also cheeses to the captain who was in Saul's camp at the valley of Elah and at war with the Philistines. David was not invited to fight with Saul's army against the Philistines because he was too young to be recruited into the Israeli army.

At his arrival to the camp, he learned of the insult by the Philistine giant against the children of Israel, but there was no one to fight against them. Saul's army had been reduced to nothing. They were fear stricken and dismayed because of the Philistines' army. Saul himself had also run out of ideas.

David managed to talk his way through to Saul, the king of Israel, and hear his concern about fighting against the giant

Goliath from Gath. Come to think of it, there was nothing that Saul could do to stop David from his big ideas. One, he himself was afraid of the giant, and two, there was no one at the Israeli camp who was ready to risk his life against Goliath. Without fighting the Philistine giant, all Israel were going into captivity at Gath, where they would serve the Philistine god Dagon.

David, being unstoppable, convinced Saul that he had been able to kill both bears and lions and that the Philistine giant was going to be just one more of his victims. Victory to David meant victory to the whole of Israel and their God. He was relying on the same God who delivered the lion and the bear into his hands to deliver Goliath into his hands. Saul tried to arm David with his own war amour, the best that he could do to show that he cared, but David did not wear it as he went out to face Goliath.

Come to think of it, if the amour could protect or strengthen David, why did Saul not use it himself? It is always better to ask God for direction than to try and fight with your human intelligence and fall flat on your face. Scripture says the arm of the flesh shall fail us. It is always better to cloth yourself with what God provides for protection than what the world has to offer. Victory comes to those who release their faith in what their God has offered.

When the Philistine saw David, he disdained him because he was a youth and cursed David by his gods. When we look at what David said, it will help us to understand why he had the victory. Remember if you have faith in God you will speak, for faith speaks. David realized the power of words, and therefore began to speak. The first statement was that "I come to you in the name of the Lord of Hosts, the God of the armies of Israel whom thou have defied".

Here David acknowledged that his strength and power came from God. This indicated that there was a force behind him. Secondly, he said "This day the Lord will deliver you into my hands". This third statement was, "I will smite thee"; fourthly, "I will take your head from thee"; fifthly, "I will give the carcasses of the host of the Philistines this day to the fowls of the air and to the wild beasts".

David's bold declaration indicated that, with God on his side, victory was eminent. David knew that victory would come when he acted upon the words that he himself had declared. It was not time to sit and wait for something to happen as we always do after praying instead of acting on the word. Remember, God moves with those who move. God said to Joshua any place that the sole of his feet shall tread he will give it to him. It wasn't going to happen if Joshua stood in one place waiting for a miracle to happen. There was the need to move and act upon the word. We need to understand that miracles follow us as we act upon the word.

With no amour and weapons David made haste to the Philistine giant. With a stone and a string he smote the Philistine giant and killed him. He stood upon the giant, took his sword from the sheath, and cut off his head.

Victory always comes to those who step out in faith and declare what they believe. Faith always speaks. When you search the Scriptures from the book of Genesis to the book of Revelation you will realize that most of the things that God did, he first spoke about them. Confess what you believe and it will come to pass. Just as we do not understand how a seed sown germinates so also is it with the words that we speak. They work, but how no one knows. Words are powerful force that works on our members. Never underestimate the power of words. They will either set you on high or bring you down. David's faith in God and in himself, along with his determination and courage, brought victory to him and to the whole of Israel.

Daniel three's friends (Daniel 3: 13-30)

A quick glance at the book of Daniel, chapter three, will throw more light to the subject in question. This was a time in the life of three Jews who were more or less condemned to death because they refused to worship an image that was set up by king Nebuchadnezzar of Babylon. For the last chance, the king questions them if they would change their mind when they hear the sound of the cornet, flute, harp, sackbut, psaltery, dulcimer, and all kind of music. Their simple answer was that the God whom they serve was able to deliver them from the burning fiery furnace. He was also able to deliver them from the hands of King Nebuchadnezzar. They made the king aware that even if their lives were spared they would not serve his gods and neither would they worship the image that he had set up.

These statements were the bold declaration of what they believed. No one was going to deprive them of their faith. If that is what they believed in then, they had to declare it. After these statements they were cast into the fire, but funny enough the fire could not consume them. The fire had no power over them. Not a hair of their head was singed, and neither were their coats changed nor did the smells of fire pass on them. The three men's faith was able to change the words of Nebuchadnezzar and to deliver them from the fire. We need to know whom we serve and take him at his word. They confessed what will happen and it came to pass. Make your declaration of the word, and it will surely come to pass. God is watching over his word to perform. Human authority can never hinder the word of faith from his servants.

The woman with the issue of blood (Mark 5: 25-34)

We should also bear in mind the woman who suffered twelve years with issue of blood from her body. The Bible says she spent all that she had but continued to grow worse. The Scriptures say that, when she heard about Jesus, she come in the press and touched his garment. But before doing this, she said to herself, "If I may touch but his clothes, I shall be whole". The Bible indicates that, after she said this, straightway the fountain of her blood was dried up and she felt in her body that she was healed of that plague.

There is always the need to speak to the mountain. Mark 11: 23 says, "For verily I say unto you that whosoever shall say unto this mountain, be thou removed, and be thou cast into the sea, and shall not doubt in his heart, but shall believe that those things which he said shall come to pass, he shall have whatsoever he said". The woman had faith in her own words and acted on them. If you believe and say it, then it shall come to pass.

The scriptures make it clear that words are like seeds that we sow on the ground. We know that any seed that is sown germinates and bears fruits. As to how this works no one knows, but it works and it has continued to work since creation until now. So also is the word that comes out of our mouth like a seed. Whenever we speak we are sowing seeds, which will surely germinate and bear fruits based on what we have spoken. Remember it worked for Abraham, for David, for the three Jews who were in captivity in Babylon, and for the woman who had an issue of blood for twelve years, so surely it will work also for you. Your faith will work, so also your fears. We need to watch what we say, since our life depends on it.

Do not despise small beginnings

Success does not just happen overnight. It takes time to build a city, and it takes time for a seed sown to germinate and bear fruits. With faith and patience, the promise or the dream will come to pass. Only remember to work out your dreams with faith and determination. Success doesn't necessary come to those who have a fat wallet. Success comes to those who gradually work with whatever they can lay their hands on with good business practice.

Even if we don't know where to start, we can draw inspiration from the successful men and women of the Bible. It was not with thousands of soldiers that Gideon won victory over the Midianites, but with three hundred men who believed that victory was within their reach. With the right mindset, determination, and teamwork, victory would come. In the time of Gideon, people who were fearful and afraid were not allowed to go to the mount of Gilead. It was not because with many there could be no success, but what good is it if they are afraid? People whose hearts are melted with fear will always draw you back in your journey to success. Where do you have your mindset? Is it to win or to lose? It is not necessary with more that victory comes but, with those who have faith in themselves.

Fear would destroy your vision.

For Joshua to be able to lead the people of Israel to the promised land God compelled him to be strong and courageous. Joshua was to achieve this by meditating on the word of God day and night. That meant getting the word of God in his system every day of his life. If you have the word, then you can speak it. Out of the abundance of the heart, the mouth will speak. This is what brings success. Most people are abounding in their vision not because it is too big or too small but because of fear. They don't have that determination that can set them on high.

The defeat of Jericho (Joshua 6: 1-20)

The verse one of Joshua chapter six says, "Now Jericho was strictly shut up because of the children of Israel; none went out and none came in". Any time I read this scripture I begin to wonder why a city should put her people into prison because of others. It all stems out of fear of the people of Israel. Jericho heard about what the Lord had done for the people of Israel in opening the Red Sea and also the river Jordan for them to cross. They also feared them because of what they did to the two kings of the Amorites that was on the other side of the Jordan namely Sihon and OG. Rahab said, "Their heart was melted with fear neither was there remaining any more courage in any man for the Lord your God who is in heaven above and the earth beneath". This was the very reason why Jericho was completely destroyed. The people of Jericho had no faith in themselves. The victory of Israel served as an intimidation to the Canaanites. It destroyed their strength and their sense of focus. What more could they do than to shut the city gates to stop its citizens from going out and strangers from coming in. This situation could have been avoided. This is what I call man-made prison. Israel therefore capitalized on their enemies' fear and moved in faith to achieve the victory they strongly sort for.

We have all been given a measure of faith, but it depends on how we use it. For fear, many of us have become prisoners in our own homes. Fear has crippled our finances. Fear has bought us diseases that have taken hold of our bodies. Our businesses are not progressing the way they should because we turn around and look at our friends' businesses prospering and then we rule ourselves out of the race. Why should someone else's success stop you from your own vision. Their vision is not your vision. Their success or failure is not necessarily you success or failure.

If we are to believe in ourselves, we will always have the victory that we seek. Don't allow other people or situations count you out of the race set before you. I have said it and will repeat it: if you don't run your race no one will do it for you. Your vision is entirely yours. The better you display your vision, the faster others would run with it. Don't let fear bring you down and destroy your vision. Put your faith to work.

Always remember that fear is your greatest enemy in your business. This could be the reason why God in his mercy admonished his people 365 times in his word that we should not fear. If God in his word encourages us not to fear for he is with us, why do we run scared when situation becomes unbearable? We should not despise a small beginning for the end shall be good. Gideon was instructed to go to battle with those who lapped water with their hand and not those who lapped water with their tongue as a dog. Remember the tongue has its functions, as does the pen of writer, not as an instrument replacing the hand. We need to realize that those who lapped water with their hands are those who are able to stay alert and able to see when the enemies are coming. The tongue is needed to declare victory of what we speak. Those who stay focused in whatever they do receive the victory they seek. A double-minded person is always unstable in all his ways. Such a person should not expect anything good.

No matter how big or small your resources are, when you stay focused and you are determined to succeed, you would prosper in all your ways. Not only was Gideon admonished not to fear but also make a move by going into the camp of the enemy. This is what is known as faith in action. There is no point in saying you can't, if you don't move or take action on what you believe. If what is in your heart is what you believe then go for it. Speak it out. Take action to your faith.

What a great instrument we are if we are in Christ. Jeremiah 51: 20-22 says:

> You are my battle-ax and weapons of war; for with you I will break the nation in pieces; with you I will destroy kingdoms, with you I will break in pieces the horse and its rider, with you I will break in pieces the chariot and its rider. With you I will break in pieces man and woman; with you I will break in pieces old and young; with you I will break in pieces the young man and the maiden.

In speaking through the prophet, Jeremiah, God said his people are his "battle axe" and "weapons of war". He promised to use us to defeat the enemy that comes against us. He said with us he would destroy nations and kingdoms, the horse and its rider; man and woman; young and old. When we make ourselves available, then God will use us for his purposes, not necessarily with multitude but with us victory will come. Our willingness to go will make the difference.

The word of the Kingdom for salvation did not come by multitude but by twelve who were carefully selected, trained, equipped, and sent out. With the twelve the gospel of the Kingdom is today all over the world. What makes the difference was that these twelve were willing and obedient. They heard miracles; they saw miracles; they were thought miracles; and so they also worked miracles. They saw in Jesus' ministry that he spoke and healed many, so they also spoke and healed many. They saw the dead being raised from the dead, so they also raised the dead. When we realize who we are, that with us God would do miracles, then we would also do miracles.

When we move, God will also move to bring the victory that we desire. Remember from the Scripture with five loaves of bread and two fishes that the Lord Jesus fed five thousand men, excluding women and children. They never challenged that the bread was not enough or the fish were too small, but in obedience they moved and distributed them as instructed by the Lord. When the disciples became obedient to what Jesus said to them and began to distribute them, they witnessed a notable miracle. In our step of faith we will always witness a miracle. When you and I move, we will always see great things in our life situation. A notable miracle awaits the people of God who are ready to move under his instructions.

To what is the Kingdom of God compared to? Is it not to a mustard seed? It is the smallest of all seed, but what happens when it is sown in the ground? Is it not that plant which grows into a huge plant, that birds are able to make their nest on and feed upon? Though it is a small seed it is able to accomplish its purpose as any massive tree. We have to make the most of what we have been given—little or much—and it will certainly grow and multiply. Remember to set yourself a goal and work at it. It is surely not with a million dollars that we win, but a fear-free heart, that is ready to go places where all men dare to, knowing that the end shall be good.

Chapter 5

Knowledge of His Word

What good is faith to an individual if we do not know what it is and the importance of it to our lives? My knowledge of the word of God, my acceptance of it, and my actions that conform to the word is my faith. My faith can be little or great, it can grow and increase, can speak and call things that are not as though they were. My faith like money buys the things that I need in the Kingdom of God. The only thing that pleases God is our faith.

Let's look at what the great Apostle of the Lord Jesus, Peter, has to say about knowledge in 2 Peter 1: 1-4.

> Simon Peter, a bondservant and apostle of Jesus Christ, to those who have obtained, like precious faith with us by the righteousness of our God and saviour Jesus Christ. Grace and peace be multiplied to you in the knowledge of God and of Jesus our Lord, as His divine power has given to us all things that pertain to life and godliness, through the knowledge of Him who called us by glory and virtue, by which have been given to us exceedingly great and precious promises, that through these you may be partakers of the divine

nature, having escaped the corruption that is in the world through lust.

Peter here described the resources that believers have that will make us grow in the grace and knowledge. Our faith, which is precious, is by the righteousness of our God and saviour Jesus Christ. This righteousness that Peter spoke about is of God and not of men. Our faith in Christ gives us access to God as any other believer. It is a great resource we possess. True righteousness is of faith not of works. It is God given, and it comes when we come to know the word of God, and also do them.

Verse two says, "Grace and peace springs from the knowledge of God". The more knowledge of God we have, the better we can tap into the blessings that are associated with it. We know that the only place where we store our faith is in our heart. For it takes what is in our heart to come out when we speak. Scripture declares that out of the abundance of the heart the mouth will speak. You store the word of God in your heart, and as you speak in time of need, that matured word comes out.

Grace is defined as the unmerited favour of God. Peace is also God's willingness to use his power and ability on our behalf. God's grace and peace as a blessing is multiplied in us through the knowledge of God. The more of the word that is in our heart, the more unmerited favour of God come to our life when we use it.

Holy knowledge is defined as a special kind of knowledge that is complete. Since our knowledge of Jesus grows as we mature in faith, we will experience his grace and peace on many different occasions.

Verse three of this very Scripture indicates that His divine power is referred to as the power of his resurrection. We can also partake of this divine power if the spirit of him that raised him from the dead dwells in us. In Romans 8: 11 Paul says, "But if the spirit of Him who raised Jesus from the dead dwells in you He who raised Christ from the dead will also give life to your mortal bodies through His Spirit who dwells in you."

These divine powers also come through the knowledge of him, and this is what gives us all things. Remember that Paul made the Ephesians aware that believers are given the spirit, which is the father's promise in the day of our redemption. Believers therefore have the spirit of God inside of us. It is this spirit that quickens us the flesh profits nothing. John quotes Jesus saying the words that he speaks to us are spirit and they are life. Sure knowledge of the word increases our faith, which is a spiritual force that is in us to bring to pass the things which we desire

In Philippians 3: 7-10, 4: 13 Paul says:

> But what things were gain to me, these I have counted loss for Christ. Yet indeed I also count all things loss for the excellence of the knowledge of Christ Jesus my Lord, for whom I have suffered the loss of all things, and count them as rubbish, that I may gain Christ and be found in Him, not having my own righteousness which is from the law, but that which is through faith in Christ, the righteousness which is from God by faith. I can do all things through Christ who strengthens me.

It is one thing to know the name of the Lord, but it is another to know what the name stands for. When I know the power that is behind the name, then when I use it the power backs my words to come to fulfilment. Our righteousness is secured not merely in intellectual knowledge but in revelation knowledge of Christ, our intimate knowledge of him.

The power of his resurrection in our life is a day-to-day experience of being in Christ. Our desire should be to conform to the image of Christ. Through his death and resurrection we have been given all things that pertain to life and godliness. When we join with Jesus that is prosperity any way you look at it.

He won't until we find out that he will. Our knowledge of the word of God will help our faith to grow and increase to enable us to ask aright. We must have the knowledge of God's willingness to prosper us. This is what brings in our prosperity. In the same way, if we have knowledge that he will heal us, then we will receive our healing. It is one thing saying God could, but it is another saying God will. Faith brings us to know the will of God in our situation.

When we look at the short story in the book of Mark it will help us to understand what I mean by knowing the will of God. Mark 1: 40-42 says:

> Now a leper came to Him, imploring Him, kneeling down to Him and saying to Him "If you are willing, you can make me clean". Then Jesus, moved with compassion, stretched out his hand and touched him and said to him, "I am willing be cleansed." As soon as He had spoken, immediately the leprosy left him, and he was cleansed.

Believers need to understand that God is willing. But if you don't have the knowledge it will not happen. As we gain the knowledge of God we will have faith in that knowledge that will multiply God's willingness towards us. When you have the knowledge, faith will arise, and action to your faith through prayer, will bring the desired answers that you desire.

Romans 4: 3, 13-19 says:

> For what does the Scriptures says? Abraham believed God and it was accounted to him for righteousness. For the promise that he would be the heir of the world was not to Abraham or to his seed through the law, but through the righteousness of faith. For if those who are of the law are heirs, faith is made void and the promise made of no effect, because the law brings about wrath, for where there is no law there is no transgression. Therefore it is of faith that it might be according to grace, so that the promise might be sure to all seed, not only to those who are of the faith of Abraham, who is the father of us all (as it is written, I have made you a father of many nation) in the presence of Him whom he believed-God, who gives life to the dead and calls those things which do not exist as though they did; who, contrary to hope, in hope believed, so that he became the father of many nation, according to what was spoken, "So shall your descendants be" And not being weak in faith, he did not consider his own body, already dead (since he was about a hundred years old), and the deadness of Sarah's womb.

When Abraham believed God, it was counted to him for righteousness. He had the right standing with God, his covenant partner. Nothing was able to change the trust and obedience that Abraham had for God. Looking at the natural, there was always going to be situation for him to look back and turn from the promise of God but, the Scriptures say he did not. On the contrary he in hope believed against hope and counted him faithful the God who had called him. When it comes to the things of God, neither your age, your education, nor your colour matter.

To receive from the Kingdom we need to use God's system, and God's system is to speak his word. When you visit a nation, it is the nation's currency that you can use to purchase anything that you want. So also in the Kingdom of God we need the Kingdom currency to acquire the essentials that we need. Faith can be said to be this currency of the kingdom. Just as we operate the worldly system with worldly principles we operate the kingdom with kingdom principles.

In 1 John 4: 4, John says, "You are of God, little children, and have overcome them, because He who is in you is greater than he who is in the world."

Believers are of God. The one in us is the Spirit of God. We have been sealed with the Spirit of God in the day of our redemption. The one out in the world is the Devil. If God be for us, who then can be against us? If we desire blessings from the kingdom then we need to seek them from the kingdom and not from this world. Apply the kingdom principles to receive from the kingdom.

Luke 18: 1-8 says:

> Then He spoke a parable to them that men always
> ought to pray and not lose heart, saying, "There
> was in a certain city a judge who did not fear God
> nor regard man. Now there was a widow in that
> city; and she came to him saying, 'Get justice
> for me from my adversary.' And he would not
> for a while; but afterward he said within himself,
> 'Though I do not fear God nor regard man yet
> because this widow troubles me I will avenge
> her, lest by her continual coming she weary
> me.'" Then the Lord said, "Hear what the unjust
> judge said. And shall God not avenge His own
> elect who cry out day and night to him, though
> He bears long with them? I tell you that he will
> avenge them speedily. Nevertheless, when the
> son of Man comes, will He really find faith on
> the earth?"

We should not forget this woman who realized the importance
of persistence, when she knew there was someone who could
change her situation around and never gave up. This woman
did not consider the wicked nature of the judge. Her focus was
only on the answer. She persisted until the answers she sought
came. With persistency we will achieve our goals, the goals
that we have set ourselves.

Mark 11: 23 helps us to realize that, if you believe, you will
speak. Faith without works is dead. One thing we need to
realize is that faith does not work for whosoever, but whosoever
shall say. If you have faith, you will speak to your situation
and your circumstances what you desire, and it will come to

pass. To operate in the kingdom one needs to apply the kingdom principles by speaking the word. Saying it involves working it.

For a moment read Proverbs 13: 12, 13, 16, which says, "Hope deferred makes the heart sick, But when the desire comes, it is a tree of life. He who despises the word will be destroyed, but he who fears the commandment will be rewarded. Every prudent man acts with knowledge but a fool lays open his folly"

Desire is like tree of life, you are destroyed when you despise the word. Reward comes to those who fear the command. What do I lose in having the word of God living big in the inside of me? My reward depend on it so also my life.

Proverbs 13: 2 says, "A man shall eat well by the fruit of his mouth, but the soul of the unfaithful feed on violence."

Believers enjoy the fruit of their mouth. My question would be what kind of fruit does your mouth produce? Remember, it would be based on what is in your heart. The Scriptures make it clear that out of the abundance of the heart the mouth will speak. What you declare today is as a result of what you stored up in your heart yesterday.

This is what Solomon the son of David has to say in Proverbs 2: 1-6:

> My son, if you receive my words, and treasure my commands within you, So that you incline your ear to wisdom; And apply your heart to understanding; Yes, if you cry out for discernment, And lift up your voice for understanding, If you seek her as silver And search for her as for hidden treasures, Then you will understand the fear of

the Lord, And find the knowledge of God. For the LORD gives wisdom; from His mouth come knowledge and understanding.

What would you do if gold nuggets were found on your land without measure?

Remember, the word of God is more than gold and diamond. Let it be implanted in your heart so you can fall back on it in time of need. For David to cry out that the Lord was his Shepherd he knew what he had his source. Remember, it was the same David who said blessed is the man who does not walk in the council of the ungodly, nor stands in the path of sinners, nor sits in the seat of the scornful, but his delight is in the law of the Lord, and in His law he meditates day and night, he shall be like a tree planted by the rivers of water, that brings forth its fruit in its season, whose leaf also shall not wither, and whatever he does shall prosper. He acts with knowledge.

David had the word of God in him. He fell upon it any time the need arose. David was one man in the Scriptures who went backward and forward requiring God as to what to do in any given situation that was confronting him. Having the word in you will prosper you. Your leaf will never wither. At the right time you will always bring forth your fruit. Why? It is all because you will know what to say at the right time to bring forth the spiritual increase the Scriptures promises.

Deut. 28: 1, 2 says:

> Now it shall come to pass, if you diligently obey the voice of the Lord your God, to observe carefully all his commandment which I command you today, that the Lord your God will set you

high above all nations of the earth. And all these blessings shall come upon you and overtake you, because you obey the voice of the Lord your God.

"Harken" means to hear intelligently and "diligently" means to declare wholly louder and louder. When we hear the word of God we need to declare it louder and louder. How can we declare something that we do not believe in it? It is only when you strongly believe that you declare it louder and louder with all convictions.

Chapter 6

The Ten Most Important Laws of Success

I don't know how successful you are or and how successful you want to be. I strongly believe that those who practice the following ten laws or rules in relation to success will surely succeed. If these rules have worked for a whole lot of people, they will definitely work for you if you put them into practice.

1. Set your goals

Remember, you can only set up goals if you know where you want to go and what you want to achieve. If you don't know where you are going, any road would lead you there. When the Israelites set out from Egypt to the land of Canaan they knew where they wanted to go even though they did not know the way and how to get there. Yes, it was not an easy task, but when they got to Canaan, they realized that they have reached their destination. Set up goals will serve as a guide to your destination. Always make sure the goals are measurable. When the goals set are measurable, you should not deviate from it. Surely others would be drawn to your vision if they can measure it.

Make sure the goals are also achievable. There is no need to set up goals that you yourself doubt can be achieved. Also, do not set up goals that require no effort. A goal that requires no effort is no goal at all.

This reminds me of a husband and a wife who decided to build a hotel. In the eyes of men it was an impossible task. Looking at their finances it was not up to scratch for them to secure a loan or support from their family. Their business background did not even warrant raising cash from other banks. There was no way anyone thought they could succeed. The only convincing proof was that they had a measurable goal, and they realized that it was achievable. Being convinced of their vision, they prayed and began to work at it. People tried to talk them out of it, whilst others tried to discourage them, saying it was an impossible dream. What kept them going was the faith in themselves that this dream will surely come to pass. They did not doubt themselves, but kept encouraging themselves. They said they trusted the God who had begun the good work in them to bring it to fulfilment. They had faith in the promise of God, and their dream came to pass. Today, they have their dream hotel.

We should always remember that there is no one that can live our dream for us. Your dream is your dream, and that makes you unique. Have a dream and see to it that it comes to pass. Believe in yourself to bring it to a perfect conclusion.

2. Write down your goals or vision

There is a very important quote in the book of Habakkuk 2: 2-3. It reads: "And the Lord answered me, and said, 'Write the vision, and make it plain on tablets, that he may run who reads it. For the vision is yet for an appointed time, but at the end it will speak, and it will not lie. Though it tarries, wait for it, because it will surely come. It will not tarry.'" Our goals need to be written down to remind us all the time. Not only do we need to stay focused but we need also to remind others to steer the course without diversions. We surely need people to accomplish this vision, and this can be made possible when they also know the route.

Many people are not fulfilled in life because they do not write down their goals, dreams, and visions. Writing down your vision helps you to stay focused. You cannot be moving from one vision to another until you have accomplished the first one.

James 1: 8 reads "For let not that man suppose that he will receive anything from the Lord; he is a double-minded man, unstable in all his ways." A double-minded person is unstable in all his ways and cannot therefore achieve anything good. With single mindedness, one can steer dreams to fulfilment. Writing it down will help you to stay focused. Writing the vision down will also draw people to help to bring it to pass. People cannot help unless they know the vision. Agendas can change; finances run high or low; strength can increase and decrease, but never change your vision or the goals that you have written down. Writing your dreams down always helps to keep them alive.

3. Get a qualification and training

Getting a qualification and training are very important if you are going to make it in life. One obstacle to success in business is when one fails to seek advice into an unknown sector of his or her business. Just as I said earlier on, that no single individual has got it altogether. Training is therefore very essential in achieving success in business. Whenever you find yourself lacking in knowledge and skills in accomplishing a given task, please *seek* the advice and training necessary.

There is always the need to study and gain the necessary knowledge for a given profession. Second Timothy 2: 15 says, "Be diligent to present yourself approved to God, a worker who does not need to be ashamed, rightly dividing the word of truth".

We always need to improve upon the skills that we have by studying all the time. Learning has to be progressive for better results. Timothy was going to be bold in his presentation of the gospel if he spent time in the Scriptures.

When the knowledge necessary is acquired through proper training, it enhances the goals that you have set up. Not only do you need to be trained, but even professional advice in your field would also do the magic necessary. Don't try to live other's dreams, but draw from their experience and expert's advice to carry you through. Footballers and boxers use videos of their opponents to draw tactics and inspiration from in order to be able to defeat them. Where necessary seek professional advice but make sure you pay them well. That means you should seek the best.

4. Know your recipe very well and improve upon it

One golden rule to your success is not to set up goals in an area where you have no clue of the recipe. I have worked in the hospitality industry for twenty-five years, and I have come to know the importance of recipe to a chef. All top chefs make it their bible and continue to improve upon it. Master a formula and always strive to improve upon it, and also derive a new one. Your successes depend on how good your recipe is. When you study medicine, you become a doctor and not an engineer. So also do you study cooking to become a chef and not a lawyer. Whatever goal you set yourself, study to have the recipe for your success. This is always very useful when you are young and choosing a career. Since your future and success depend on it, please choose carefully. Know what your talents are for it is easy to improve upon them through training.

5. Always have success mindset

Make up your mind daily that you *will* succeed. Most people quit when situations become unbearable. Let me remind you that most of the successful people you see around you did not succeed the first time they started. They encountered problems and difficulties; however, they did not give up but hung in there until success came to them. So don't quit when you encounter difficulties. Success comes to those who persist through trials and difficulties. Life is full of ups and downs. For every flat plain there will be hills and valleys. Life would be boring if it was success all the time. Persistence brings reward, but quitters never make it to their destination. Being blessed can be hard work. Success comes with a price tag. Remember, you cannot be successful if you are reluctant to pay the price.

6. Let your money work for you by controlling your finances

What makes you think the nine to five jobs that you pursue day in and day out, running after buses and trains and tubes, will bring you? Never spend all your time working for money. Millionaires do not work for money as most of us do. Their money works for them. Due to our poor management of money or our cash flow we are always running to and from chasing money, but we are never satisfied with money. Money seems to delude us. Learn how you can make the little that comes in work for you. The weekly money that you earn, when properly managed, that will build up into the millions that you seek.

It is never too late to start where you are now. Learn how to invest in shares that will bring proper dividends. Invest in a business that will bring in profits. Let the asset column of your business exceed the liabilities column. This can be done by keeping you spending to the minimum and by protecting and preserving assets. Let your profits buy the luxuries and not your capital. Play the game of cash flow very well, avoiding unnecessary expenses. Never underestimate your outflow; it is that which can bring you down. Whenever necessary, reinvest any money that comes into your pocket. Every penny counts. Always try as much as possible to manage your cash flow. Budget before you spend. Don't just buy because you need it. In the United Kingdom 90 per cent of the items that foreigners buy to ship back home when they retire becomes rubbish by the time they get to their destination. What is the point in buying stock that you don't need now but for the future? This money could be well invested and the profit reinvested for the grand money that could help you make it in life when you retire.

Be ready to train yourself where necessary in order to gain the necessary confidence that you desire, so that the increase that comes your way can be controlled. Most people's problem is not the lack of money but how to manage money. There are people whose income per month is great, but due to their lack of financial management skills are not able to save, not even for rainy days. Until the outflow equates the inflow one, is bound to have a financial crisis. If what comes in, little or much, is managed, there will always be leftovers. I have come to realize that most people's problem is not lack of money in their system but lack of simple mathematics. Simple addition and subtraction are still unknown to many people. Don't get me wrong they can be great mathematicians in books but not in reality. When it comes to finances most of these mathematicians are nowhere to be found. They are lost in the simple equation of adding and subtraction. Remember what goes out of your finances as spending doesn't come back. Simply remember that what is spent reduces your totals. Learn how to spend money wisely.

Wherever your financial circumstances may stand, now is the time to change where you are. One step at a time, and the victory would come. Focus on what God has called you to do. If it is as a housewife, manage the home in faith. If as a teacher, teach with all your heart and mind in faith. If it is as a doctor, conduct your practice all in faith as a servant of the Lord. If it is as a business man or woman, manage the business. Who is going to do it if you don't? Do what you know to do best in faith, and the good Lord would add the rest. The ordained spiritual force in the Genesis account will always be yours. Don't try to be what you are not. You are not somebody else, and you can never be someone else. You are unique. There is no one of your kind here on earth or the one to come.

Remember, you are special. You are what God has made you to be. Your uniqueness can not be replaced, be marched, or be compromised. Therefore no one can replace the role that you have been destined for. Your God given individualism cannot be replaced. Your ability, your resources, and your contribution to humanity will always be lacking if you don't take your position in this life. We all need each other, as we all complement each other. Humanity as a whole will be lacking if you as an individual refuse to play you part or role on earth.

7. Choose your friends and heroes carefully

Associate yourself with people who will motivate, listen and encourage you, not those who will criticize and discourage you. There is power in association. In most cases, friends complement each other. It is always easy to know someone if you know his best friend. Bear it in mind that fearful and poor people will always talk you down and bring you to their world and destroy your goals and vision. Let your friends lift you up in the vision that you share with them.

The power of a mentor is so essential in your success. Choose your mentors carefully making sure they are people who would help you to deliver and achieve your goals. Look at their history and their achievements and learn from them. Choose winners and not losers. Joshua chooses Moses, Elisha chooses Elijah, Peter chooses the Lord Jesus, Silas chooses Paul, and they all saw victory. If you want victory, then chose the right mentor

8. Make sure you pay yourself

This is one of the most difficult principles of success. Though it is difficult, it is the most important. If you work all your life but fail to pay yourself at the end of the week or month, you will retire with nothing. You need to make sure that at the end of each month you set aside for yourself a minimum of 10 per cent of whatever comes in. Whether salaries, bonuses, or gifts you need to pay oneself 10 per cent. Remember, paying yourself first comes before paying your bills, mortgage, shopping, credit cards, and insurance.

To be able to pay yourself first you need to keep your expenses and debts to the minimum. Always avoid high credit-card bills on which you have to pay high interest. Make sure you buy only what is necessary for your upkeep and not unnecessary gadgets and clothing. When it comes to buying, shop around and buy reasonably. Remember that money spent would never come back. You should bear it in mind that money that is not spent properly is your own strength down in the drain. What is the point of having your wardrobe full of clothing that you use only once in a year and can also be substituted. If there is anything in your wardrobe that you have not used in the last eighteen months it indicates that you don't need it. Sell it now and invest the money, and that money can be reinvested.

Paying yourself first will inspire you to go out and create more money that can be reinvested. This can be done by setting aside 10 per cent of whatever comes in. If you seek success, then start paying yourself and let the profit buy the luxuries. This is not an impossible task but a desire that has to be nurtured to bring financial success. Remember, it comes first in all your expenses. This is one important way to grow your capital if you are starting from scratch. The desire to grow rich begins here, so as to avoid working all your life to the grave.

9. Be motivated and determined to be successful

Success comes only when you are committed and have the passion to cross the finish line. Winning is for winners. Winning will cost you in terms of pleasure, luxuries, loneliness, criticism, pressure, and sacrifice. As good as it feels to be affirmed and applauded, at some point in time you need to stop and ask yourself, how much I am willing to sacrifice. As you are in love with success you need to count the cost of succeeding. Always be motivated and know that you can make it to your destination. Be determined that you will cross the finish line no matter what. Success is not based on what or where you start but where and how you cross the finish line. To succeed you need to give it what it takes. Remember, it takes hard work, not folding of alms, not waiting for someone to lead you, not looking back or waiting to check if the crowds are coming. It is your life and your future that is at stake. When you move, God will move with you.

10. Remember to give

The law of giving and receiving will always work as long as the heavens remain. This is a spiritual law, and it also works in the natural realm. Just as the seed that we plant on the ground germinates and bears fruit not knowing how, so also do the things that you give bear fruits. If the seed sown yields after its kind, so also does what you say. The law of giving and receiving works perfectly with everyone. Some of the increase would be thirty times, some sixty times and others a hundred times, all depending on what ground you sow.

I have grown to realize that, when you love, you will be loved; when you teach, you will be taught; when you feed, you will be fed; when you hate, you will be hated; so also when you give, you will be given. If you want anything in this world, first give, and it shall be given back to you.

My visit to Israel thought me my greatest lesson in giving. They that only receive but not give are like the Dead Sea, which has no life living in it, because when it receives a supply of water from the River Jordan, it never gives away or shares with other rivers or lakes. But the Sea of Galilee is full of life, because when it receives a supply of water from other rivers, it gives some away.

When a seed is kept for so long without being sown, it rots. Seeds are meant to be eaten or sown. Therefore if you want to reap the full benefit of your seed then you have to sow it or eat it. What good is a seed if the full benefit is not received? Your seed is meant to bring forth the desired increase, when it is sown in the right place.

Chapter 7

The Power of the Law of Navigation

If you don't know where you are going any road would led you there. There is always one way to your destination, but it takes a leader to chart the course. Charting the course always requires proper planning. Do you want to succeed in business, in education, in employment, in leadership, or in the ministry? You need to set time aside to plan. In planning, attention to detail is essential. From start to finish every detail should be covered and executed accordingly. All equipment, personnel, timescale, resources, and eventualities that may happen need to be planned for.

Attention to team preparation is essential. Enough time is necessary for preparation and planning that is made to avoid a last-minute decision. Proper planning gives followers the sense of direction to follow through the vision and the dream that you set yourself.

A good leader always stays focused and is ready for all eventualities that come his or her way. They line themselves up to be able to deal with situation rather than situation controlling them. Your followers need to know your vision for them in order to established their destination and what it will take to get there. It also helps to recruit the right staff for the success of the business. Proper planning also helps to recognize hindrances before they appear in the horizon.

As a leader, what do you see and when do you see it? A leader sees more than those that he is leading. He sees further than all and always sees before any other person. With this in mind he is able to deal with the situation before obstacles take control over the business.

A good leader always realizes that people depend on them for their direction, and therefore his ability to chart the course is essential. Whatever decision is made by a leader will either be life or death; top or bottom; success or failure; profit or loss; large crowd or small crowd. Victory should always be every leader's dream. The ultimate goal of a good leadership is success. It is success that helps a leader to learn more about himself and whether he is capable or incapable of his duties. Past success could be drawn on, but past failures should never be forgotten to avoid defeat.

A good leader always learns from his mistakes. People who keep on committing the same error every time should remember that they are hampering their own progress.

Effective navigation always starts with experience

Never forget that your past alone is not a guarantee of your success. No matter how much you learn from your past, it will never tell you all you need to know for the present if you fail to learn from your mistakes.

There is also the need to learn from the team leadership or other organization. Learn to listen and heed advice where necessary. A good leader needs a mentor—a mentor who can spend time with you.

As a leader, always examine the situation before you commit yourself. You need to count the cost before committing others or yourself. All decisions made should bring about the desired result of the dream.

Some questions and answers

First, ask yourself a few questions. Do you have the desire and the faith in yourself to succeed? Secondly, are you sure you will get to your destination with the team that you have selected? Thirdly, what about your leadership team? Leadership can make or break the vision, if you are not careful. The team should buy into your vision and run with it. Leaders should have faith in themselves and also other members of the team. Where there is fear and intimidation the vision will be delayed and sometimes not come to pass.

A leader's self-deception will cost him the vision. When you trust your own vision and believe in yourself, others will help to bring it to pass. Having faith in your dreams will help you when it comes to planning, which brings the vision to fulfilment. Leaders should bear in mind that one of the major barriers to successful planning in any given situation will be fear, ignorance of the unknown future, and lack of leadership imagination.

Remember, a vision is not accepted, supported, or rejected on the basis of size or timescale but on the size of the leader.

When proper preparation is done and confidence and trust is conveyed to the people, a dream or a vision would be accepted and come to pass.

Our study on the law of navigation will be incomplete unless we spend time to study the Lord Jesus's way of navigation. His goal was to draw all men to himself in the Kingdom. He states all the vision in the book he has given. He realized the vision was for an appointed time but proper planning was the key to success. He started by choosing the twelve apostles out of the multitude. Yes, the multitude could be perfect for the task ahead but only for a short time unless proper planning and training were given. The twelve who he selected, trained, and equipped were more than qualified to do the work. He was a mentor to the twelve. Leadership was by example. He invested his time and energy in them. He lived, ate, and slept with them. He travelled, preached, and performed miracles with them. He always applied the doctrine and principles of the Kingdom to their daily lives. They in turn were able to convey the message of the Kingdom to many after his death, and through that many have come to the revelatory knowledge of Christ.

A bank clerk is trained with real money during his or her training season so that when he comes in contact with counterfeit on the job it becomes easy to detect. On-the-job training equips the staff to be strong and well acquainted with the necessary requirements of the vision. First-hand experience is therefore very necessary. When we look into Jesus's inner circle, we see that these were men who bought into the vision more than the rest of the team. The inner circles are those that we will here refer to as the executive team or directors. In Jesus's case it was Peter, James, and John. The three worked perfectly with the Lord, and so should the executive team with the visionaries. The three worked also very well with the twelve; the twelve with the seventy; and the seventy with the five hundred. With proper training and preparation the Lord's name has reached the entire world. With proper law of leadership one is bound to get to wherever he wants to get to without any limitation. The only limitation to our success in this life is ourselves.

Remember, as a leader you can easily be intimidated by other similar groups of businesses, your own management team, and even suppliers. But why should you be brought down by others? It is your dream and vision, so you are the only one who can say you will win or lose. The only thing the leader should bear in mind is that the vision comes to pass with much business. Remember to work at the vision and equally know without reasonable doubt that it shall come to pass. When you are not happy with your suppliers, sack them. If the product is not the right one, demand it to be changed. Remember, you are paying for the goods and services, so make sure you have the right service.

The management team does not dictate to you but are given directives by you. Learn to work with your leaders for the common goal. Pay them well in order to get the best results. If you desire to succeed, then you need to pay the price. Success can sometime cost you your friends, your family, your sleep, your pleasure, and even your joy. Running away is not the way forward, but hanging in there is. A leader who knows where he is going always succeeds in his business.

Chapter 8

Success Through Teamwork in Business

Teamwork begins with you as the leader and the team that you set yourself to work with. This reminds me of a verse in the book of Leviticus 26: 8 which reads, "Five of you will chase a hundred, and a hundred of you will chase ten thousand and your enemies will fall by the sword before you". This Scripture helps us to understand what an organized army of workers does in any given situation. What one can achieve two can achieve even ten times better.

When you visit a production line in a factory where there are individuals doing their own thing and a line where a team is in place coordinating their task accordingly, then you will understand the importance of teamwork. One can chase a thousand, but remember two can chase ten thousand, which is equally true in business. Your business is bound to succeed if there is a coordinating effort of teamwork. I have worked with a team of individuals who were equally good in their field of work, but the result cannot be compared to a team that I had in another establishment that worked as a team. Wherever there is a team spirit the achievement is outstanding. When all the wheels of the team are in place and working together there is victory. The people who have come together to work as a team should have the team spirit. I always advise people to work individually where team spirit is lacking. Lack of team spirit is always a recipe for disaster in a given work place.

There is no better illustration of teamwork than that which exists between migratory birds such as geese. One would hardly see one goose flying alone. They fly in groups of up to twenty-five members and sometimes more. With teamwork, they are able to fly for from one continent to another, a distance which no single bird can do on its own. Geese fly in v-formation known as a skein. They work as a team, which greatly boosts the efficiency and the range they fly. With the v-formation it is only the leaders who face the headwind, but the up wash from the wingtip vortices helps the bird ahead. The up wash as the first bird flips its wings assists each bird in sustaining its own weight in the flight, just as a glider is able to maintain its height through the rising air. With teamwork each bird is able to achieve a reduction in induced drag, and gain velocity of up to 70 per cent. As a team, the birds at the tips of the formation and the one in front rotate in a cyclical fashion to spread the fatigue during the flight.

Their v-formation also helps the birds to make proper coordination and communication and allow the birds to maintain eye contact with each other with an unobstructed field of vision. Hence, it helps to avoid or fight all impending dangers that may confront them. It also helps to keep track of each bird in the team. A study indicates that a goose fling alone will have higher heart rates than when they fly in teams. Flying in groups helps to conserve energy.

When a goose become too weak to fly with the group it is not left alone, but two members of the group are dispatched to stay with it until it recovers to join the group or dies. They take care of the weak because they are in it together.

This is what I call teamwork. On a football team there are defenders, midfielders, and strikers, and these three groups have to work together to achieve any goals. Whilst the defenders make sure that the goal and the back is protected against incoming balls, and the midfielders make sure they get the ball to the strikers, who have to score to win a game. Here teamwork is very essential. So also do we need this in business situations.

Success through teamwork begins with proper leadership

Does the leadership team understand teamwork? Do they have a system in place to create the team spirit, which fuels the flames of the team? What type of leadership structure is in place? How does the leader distribute a given task to the team? Success or failure of a team depends on the leadership. You can have good individual prayers to form the England team, but that would be no use if they don't have a good leader to train them to work as a team. For some reason England has not been able to achieve any success in their matches since 1966 due to lack of team spirit and good leadership. Success has eluded the team not because they don't have the individual players with the skills to do the job. England has one of the best premierships competitions in the whole world, but remember it is not individuals that win matches but a team.

Participation

Do all the individuals on the team participate with one heart and mind? Do they all perform their given tasks? What good is a team if the individual members do their own thing? When a member of a team refuses to contribute his best, then the team breaks down. It is therefore essential to ask that individual to leave the team to secure victory. To win in a Formula One race is not the duty of only the driver behind the steering wheel but the team of engineers as a whole from the highest to the lowest, including the cleaner of the wind shield.

There is no more winning team than the fishermen that ply the North Sea of Scotland. They load their boats with the necessary food, drink, and equipment for the journey which lasts for about two weeks, depending upon how fast they are able to reach their target. The skipper makes sure all the crew members are up to scratch and ready to give their 100 per cent. On the sea, there is no room for complacency. Any single incident can be fatal or costly to the ship and its crew. Every member of the crew is important to the rest. The cook is equally important as the skipper himself. They make sure they cover each and everyone's back. Every role is so important that even when a member of the crew is injured he is forced to work with it. There was a time I watched and saw a crew member who lost one of his fingers and was bleeding. The next thing I saw was that this same guy had a bandage on his hands soaked in blood helping to pull home a net which had been cast hours earlier. His position was so vital that the voyage would suffer without him. It was not cruelty but commitment, fulfilling his role in the team. They travel together, cast the nets together, draw the nets together, sort and pack the catch together, and then sit and eat together. The teams that work and pull together win together.

Until you leave the comfort of the shoreline and lunch into the deep the victory, the rewards, and success that you seek will never materialize.

Objectives

On most occasions, individuals do not contribute to the team's dream. This is not intentional in most cases, but because there is no clear objective from the leader who runs the show. Where clear and proper directions are set, individuals contribute. People need to know where they are going and what their destination is. For lack of knowledge people perish. How would individuals know they have arrived if there is a lack of objectives? Goals must be set for the team. Each individual member of the team should work toward that given goal without deviation.

Planning

Initial and proper planning is necessary in a team for success. There is no success without proper planning. Planning in whatever business you have set up is very essential. Planning helps you to advance with your set goals. It gives a sense of direction as to where, how, when, and who to get to your destination. Planning is the vehicle that channels the team through each stage of the business for success. When the sight of the vision is gone, it is the initial plan that will serve as a light to your future for accomplishment. Always remember to write the vision down. Take time off your busy schedule to plan. Even if you have to go on holiday where you can have a sound mind with no interruptions, so much the better! All details to your dreams should be spelled out on paper. Though adjustments could be made, the initial plan would serve as a guide for success.

Time management

The only time we have control of is the present. Many people are very bad with the use of time. Time in all essence is money. Time lost will never be gained. Every moment in a production line of a business is very important. Well-managed time in business brings success. There should always be set time in doing things. Always use time at hand and never procrastinate. Let the time available produce the desired success for your business. The only reason we never get started is because we focus on tomorrow instead of today. Today is yours, but tomorrow you cannot put your finger on, so don't worry so much about it. The greatest time waster is the time of getting started. The hardest part of making a tough phone call is picking up the phone receiver and dialling the number. Remember the first line of a letter is the hardest, get through with it then you realize that the rest will follow. You may pray, plan, and prepare but you must step out in faith to act. Schedule time for doing what you don't like to do, and each time you follow through and do it, it would get easier and you will get better at it.

Desire

Desire is the last but not the least vehicle that will transport you to victory through teamwork. How much are you willing to sacrifice to bring to pass your dream and visions? Is it your desire to succeed or are you just trying on this business? Are there procedures in place to bring this desire to past? Do you actually have the passion to bring to pass your vision? Remember your business success is determined by your strong desire to reach the target no matter what. Not only do you need the passion yourself but also to all those in the team. The crown needs to be sorted for by all. Together we will stand. All team players need to have the same mental attitude to release the desire to strive forward for success. When all team members push and pull together there is always bound to be success and victory.

Chapter 9

God Can Change Your Situation Round

One of the most important principles we need to understand as believers is our relationship with God. There is a relationship between us and a higher being. You have been separated or set apart by God for a purpose. You don't just live for yourself. You live for a reason, which sometime is beyond your understanding. Having been set apart doesn't necessary mean things will just fall into place when you sit down and fold your hands.

Let's look at the word of God that came to the prophet Jeremiah.

Jeremiah 1: 5-12 says:

> Before I formed you in the womb I knew you, before you were born I sanctified you, I ordained you a prophet to the nations. Then said I, A Lord God! Behold I cannot speak, for I am a youth, But the Lord said to me, Do not say I am a youth, for you shall go to all to whom I send you. And whatever I command you shall you speak. Do not be afraid of their faces, for I am with you to deliver you, says the Lord. Then the Lord put forth is hand and touched my mouth, and the Lord said to me. Behold I have put my words

in your mouth. See I have this day set you over the nations and over the kingdom. To root out and to pull down, to destroy and to throw down, to build and to plant. Moreover the word of the Lord came to me saying, Jeremiah, what do you see? And I said, I see a branch of an almond tree. Then the Lord said to me, "you have well seen for I am ready to perform my word." (NKJV)

At a very critical point in the history of Israel, God needs to make His word a reality in the life of Jeremiah. To get this critical message across to His people God determined the call of Jeremiah before his conception. God knowing Jeremiah indicated knowledge that came from relationship and personal commitment. This is something that God made it clear through his divine work in setting him apart for this special service, a prophet to the people and a messenger to the kingdom. He was called to address the kings of Judah and the leaders of Babylon. Jeremiah doubted the power in him to speak before the nations with his youth, a case in which most senior people would find themselves unable to move forward.

He was not asked to go on his own power but trough the powerful presence of God and His word. Remember, it is the word of God that is living and powerful and sharper than any two-edged sword (Hebrews 4: 12). It is with the word of God that we are able to change situations around.

With the word of God, Jeremiah was able to deliver God's people, Judah, from the captors and the poor from the oppressors. God promised Jeremiah that he was with him even to deliver him from his enemies and the nation's leaders who would attack him. God put His word in Jeremiah's mouth and that was what he was ready to perform. As he became obedient and spoke the word, results came.

It is easy to take the blessings of God for granted. It is one thing being blessed, but it is another making sure the blessing materialize and continue to grow in every sector of your life. Jeremiah was the one to make sure the will of God was spoken. When you and I do the word of God, He will also make sure He watches over it to perform. John indicated that the word that God speaks to us is life and spirit (John 6: 63). When you do the word given to you, then success will come. Just as God confirmed his word to Jeremiah with visions, so he will confirm his Word to you with signs and wonders.

Like Jeremiah, Moses was also called to speak to pharaoh king of Egypt at a decisive point of Israel history. To be able to this, God has to change Moses situation around.

Exodus 2: 1-10 says

> And a man at the house of Levi went to take as wife a daughter as Levi. So the woman conceived and bore a son. And when she saw that he was a beautiful child, she hid him 3 months. But when she could no longer hide him, she took an arc of bulrushes for him dubbed it with asphalt and pitches, put the child in it and laid it in the reed by the river bank. And his sister stood a far off to know what would be done to him. Then the daughter of Pharaoh came to bathe at the river and her maidens walked alone the river side, and when she saw the arc among the reeds, she sent her maids to go and get it. And when she opened it, she saw the child, and beholds the baby wept.

So she had compassion on him, and said 'this is one of the Hebrews children'. Then his sister said to pharaoh's daughter, 'shall I go and call a nurse for you from the Hebrew women, that she may nurse the child for you?' And pharaoh's daughter said to her 'go'. So the maiden went and called the child's mother. Then pharaohs daughter said to her, 'take this child away and nurse him for me and I will give you your wages'. So the woman took the child and nursed him. And the child grew, and brought him to pharaoh's daughter and he became her son. So she called his name Moses saying, 'because I drew him out of the water'.

There were twelve tribes in Israel, but it was the house of Levi that God chose to be the priestly family for Israel. Were they better than the other eleven tribes of Israel? No, but that the Glory of God may reside with Israel His people. Moses was not the first child but he was the one that God chose to protect and commission for his service. We should always remember that each and every one of us has his or her own given direction in this life. Always walk in your God given path, and the victory will come.

Seeing he was beautiful, the mother hid Moses for three months from the authorities who sought to kill him. Not able to hide him anymore, Jochebed made an ark, which served as a means to save Moses. It was none other than pharaoh's daughter who discovered the ark and the child. Not only did God through pharaoh's daughter save Moses from the river and possible death that pharaoh commanded but also through pharaohs' treasury he provided wages to Jochebed, the child's own mother caring for her son. This alone was a miracle. Pharaoh's daughter adapted Moses as her own son, giving him a princely status. These things were done to prepare Moses for the task ahead.

Hebrews 11: 24-26 says, "By faith when Moses became of age refused to be called son of pharaohs daughter, choosing rather to suffer affliction with the people of God than to enjoy the passing pleasures of sin esteeming the reproach of Christ greater riches than the treasures in Egypt, for he looked to the reward."

Moses trusted in what God had in store for him though it came with suffering rather than the high position in pharaoh's court. He realized that if God was able to save him from drowning (pharaoh's means for all Israel's male born children to die) then He was capable enough to bring him the reward irrespective of the suffering. The reward equally motivated him to endure in the faith. In any call of God, the reward always seems to exceed the suffering that is associated with it. That Moses responded to the call of God in Midian shows clearly why God saved him when he was a child. In the book of Isaiah, God is seeking who He may send and who it is that will go.

Exodus 3: 1-10 says:

> Now Moses was tending the flock in Jethro his father in law, the priest of Midian. And he led the flock to the back of the desert and came to Horeb, the mountain of God. And the angel of the Lord appeared to him in a flame of fire from the midst of a bush. So he looked, and behold, the bush was burning wit fire, but the bush was not consumed. Then Moses said, I will now turn aside and see this great sight why the bush does not burn. So when the Lord saw that he turned

aside to look, God called to him from the midst from the bush and said 'Moses, Moses!' And he saidHere I am' then he said 'do not draw near to this place. Take your sandals off your feet, for the place where you stand his Holy ground'. Moreover he said I am the God of your father, the God of Abraham, the God of Isaac and the God of Jacob. And Moses hid his face, for he was afraid to look upon God. And the Lord said, 'I have surely seen the oppression of my people who are in Egypt, and have heard they're cry because of their taskmasters, for I know their sorrows. So I have come down to deliver them out of the hand of the Egyptians, and to bring them up from that land to a good and large land, to a land flowing with milk and honey, to the place of the Canaanites and the Hittites and the Amorites and the Perizzites and the Hivites and the Jebusites. Now therefore, behold, the cry of the children of Israel has come to me and I have also seen the oppression in which the Egyptians oppressed him. Come now, therefore, and I will send you to pharaoh that you may bring my people, the children of Israel out of Egypt. (NKJV)

Out of a desolate place (Horeb) God called His man. With God's presence, a desolate place will be a holy place that God has set apart to declare his glory, the mountain of God. It took the fire of God to draw Moses's attention due to what he went through at the beginning. God also reminded Moses that his covenant relationship with Abraham, Isaac, and Jacob was still in effect. We always need to be aware that whatever happens to us, God is aware but will never intervene until we ask Him. God saw the oppression of his people who were in Egypt. He heard their cry because of their task masters, and he knew their sorrows. He then decided to come down and deliver them out of the hands of the Egyptians. He set up a strategy to bring them to a land that was flowing with milk and homey. This was as a result of Israel crying onto God. God also gave them the land that had been inherited by their enemies. It was the land that he promised Abraham, Isaac, and Jacob as their inheritance. With Moses, God would bring Israel, the covenant people, to their inheritance. With all the excuses that Moses gave God, he availed himself and responded to the call of God, and he became great. There will always be blessings and rewards when we respond to our call. The visions and the dreams will come to pass when we work at it.

The Scripture indicates that Samuel ministered to the Lord at the time that the word of the Lord was real, and there was no widespread revelation or vision. This was a time of extremely limited prophetic activities because there were few faithful Israelites who took God at his word.

1 Samuel 1:1-11 says,

> There was a certain man from Ramathaim, a Zuphite from the hill country of Ephraim, whose name was Elkanah son of Jeroham, the son of Elihu, the son of Tohu, the son of Zuph, an Ephraimite. He had two wives; one was called Hannah and the other Peninnah. Peninnah had children, but Hannah had none. Year after year this man went up from his town to worship and sacrifice to the LORD Almighty at Shiloh, where Hophni and Phinehas, the two sons of Eli, were priests of the LORD. Whenever the day came for Elkanah to sacrifice, he would give portions of

the meat to his wife Peninnah and to all her sons and daughters. But to Hannah he gave a double portion because he loved her, and the LORD had closed her womb. And because the LORD had closed her womb, her rival kept provoking her in order to irritate her. This went on year after year. Whenever Hannah went up to the house of the LORD, her rival provoked her till she wept and would not eat. Elkanah her husband would say to her, "Hannah, why are you weeping? Why don't you eat? Why are you downhearted? Don't I mean more to you than ten sons?"

Once when they had finished eating and drinking in Shiloh, Hannah stood up. Now Eli the priest was sitting on a chair by the doorpost of the LORD's temple. In bitterness of soul Hannah wept much and prayed to the LORD. And she made a vow, saying, "O LORD Almighty, if you will only look upon your servant's misery and remember me, and not forget your servant but give her a son, then I will give him to the LORD for all the days of his life, and no razor will ever be used on his head. (NIV)

Hannah realized her circumstances of not having children and went to Shiloh to call upon the God of Israel. Even during her prayer time, the prince of Shiloh thought she was drunk. She said she was not but made her request onto God and she vowed to give her son to God. God answered her prayers and gave him a son. She dedicated her son, Samuel, to the service of the Lord. She lent him to the Lord and idea of complete giving up to the Lord. She did this because her sense of strength was in God. She realized that there was none as holy as the Lord, none beside him, and no rock like our God. Hannah also called to mind how God reverses human circumstances by humbling the proud and exalting the lowly. God breaks the bow against the mighty and those who stumble he girds with strength. He made the hungry cease from hunger and those full borrowing bread.

As Shiloh the priest Eli was old there was also Hophhni and Phinehas, sons of Eli, but it was Samuel that God called. There was then the need for the people of God to hear his voice so as to be instructed. So God called Samuel. The Scripture says the sons of Eli were corrupt, indicating they were sons of Belial people of no value. Our relationship with God makes us valuable, people of authority and power. We are able to go to places without being intimidated. When we corrupt ourselves we lose sight of the visions and also our schemes.

Samuel grew both in stature and in favour of the Lord and of men. Because Eli and his children did not honour God, he decided to honour those who will honour Him. God decided to rise up a faithful priest who should do according to what was in his heart and mind, saying, "I will build him a sure house and he shall walk before me. He shall be anointed forever." (Samuel 2: 35) 1 Samuel 3: 19-20 says so Samuel grew and the Lord was with him and let none of his word will fall to the ground. And all Israel from Dan to Beersheba knew that Samuel had been established as a prophet of the Lord. The Lord being with him was the key to Samuel's success as a prophet. God remained with him and did not allow any of his word to fall. All the prophecies God delivered through Samuel were fulfilled. When we avail ourselves, God can always change our situation around to work to our favour.

God had plans for David, who was ignored, rejected, and taken to be nobody in his own family. God instructed Samuel to go to Jesse, a Bethlehemite, and anoint one of his sons as a king over Israel.

1 Samuel 16: 1-13 says:

> The LORD said to Samuel, "How long will you mourn for Saul, since I have rejected him as king over Israel? Fill your horn with oil and be on your way; I am sending you to Jesse of Bethlehem. I have chosen one of his sons to be king."

But Samuel said, "How can I go? Saul will hear about it and kill me."

The LORD said, "Take a heifer with you and say, 'I have come to sacrifice to the LORD.' Invite Jesse to the sacrifice, and I will show you what to do. You are to anoint for me the one I indicate."

Samuel did what the LORD said. When he arrived at Bethlehem, the elders of the town trembled when they met him. They asked, "Do you come in peace?"

Samuel replied, "Yes, in peace; I have come to sacrifice to the LORD. Consecrate yourselves and come to the sacrifice with me." Then he consecrated Jesse and his sons and invited them to the sacrifice.

When they arrived, Samuel saw Eliab and thought, "Surely the LORD's anointed stands here before the LORD."

But the LORD said to Samuel, "Do not consider his appearance or his height, for I have rejected him. The LORD does not look at the things man looks at. Man looks at the outward appearance, but the LORD looks at the heart." Then Jesse called Abinadab and had him pass in front of Samuel. But Samuel said, "The LORD has not chosen this one either." Jesse then had Shammah pass by, but Samuel said, "Nor has the LORD chosen this one." Jesse had seven of his sons pass before Samuel, but Samuel said to him, "The LORD has not chosen these." So he asked Jesse, "Are these all the sons you have?"

"There is still the youngest," Jesse answered, "but he is tending the sheep."

Samuel said, "Send for him; we will not sit down until he arrives." So he sent and had him brought in. He was ruddy, with a fine appearance and handsome features.

Then the LORD said, "Rise and anoint him; he is the one." So Samuel took the horn of oil and anointed him in the presence of his brothers, and from that day on the Spirit of the LORD came upon David in power. Samuel then went to Ramah. (NIV)

Samuel was to choose and anoint one of Jesse's children who he had set apart for his service. Like Samuel, when it comes to selection we tend to look at the outward appearance and stature instead of the heart. Many Christian marriages are in shambles because we did not seek the heart of the man or the woman we married, but the beauty and stature. In business we tend toward more glamorous professions and well established ventures, leaving the very one we are talented to do. Please let us always seek what God has for us to be able to succeed. The state of man's heart is far more significant than natural ability and physical appearance. You don't judge a fruit by the colour of the skin but the juice in it.

At Bethlehem Jesse made all his seven sons to pass before Samuel with the exception of David. Having realized that God had not chosen any of them, Samuel requested if there were any more children. Remember it is God who calls and equips not us ourselves. That is why it is very important to do what God has called you to do. There is no one person that can do what God has given you to do. The accomplishment of any given task by God is in the hands of the one called.

It was David that God had in mind to rule over Israel as a king, though young, but not his brothers. The Scriptures make it clear that when Samuel anointed David in the midst of his brothers, the Holy Spirit came upon David from that day forward. The spirit ushered and empowered him into his office for service. Wherever God places us, he gives us the power and authority to do it effectively. David became king over Israel with supernatural faith in God who set him apart.

2 Chronicles 29: 26-28 says, "Thus David the son of Jesse reigned over all Israel. And the period that he reigned over Israel was forty years; seven years he reigned in Hebron, and thirty-three years he reigned in Jerusalem. So he died in a good old age, full of days and riches and honour; and Solomon his son reined in his place."

David reigned over Israel over forty years and died at a good old age. He had riches and honour and his son Solomon reigned in his stead. What a blessing in faith and obedience to God, his covenant partner.

Chapter 10

Making of a Leader

The success of a leader depends on how well he or she is accepted by those that he or she works with. A key for a leader is recognition by the people or the team. God made Israel to recognize Moses as a leader in order to be able to lead them. So also did God work signs and wonders through Joshua so that Israel would accept him as their leader. If you are not able to sell the vision to your immediate workers, then how can you make sure that they come to pass? People want to know you before they buy into your vision.

The passion and integrity of a leader's lifestyle must match his messages. Whenever your words and actions match, then you are d eemed credible by all. People would like to know if the value you are giving them is worth the price tag. Your relationship with other people will determine your buying-in level. People will like to know you through your actions and not only through your words. People will accept you if they know what is important to you, what brings you joy, and what makes you angry. You as a leader need to know your team member's cries their songs, and their dreams, which will prove to them that you care. Your staff interest should be at hand. How you treat people would determine how long and well they accept you. There is always the need to build up a relationship. Talk to your staff about current issues and what you believe. Build a relationship and do not debate about issues. Let people hear what they want to hear and address their needs.

Proper communication

a. Know your vision and communicate it very well

b. Be clear and simple

c. Communicate what you want the people to know

d. Tell them what you want them to do

e. Express to them the opportunities in it for them

f. Leave them with no doubt in their mind

g. Give them time and don't use pressure tactics

h. Discuss with the key personnel any changes to the vision

i. Remain in touch with the people, customers, staff, and the board of directors at all times.

Anticipate victory by making sure that the picture of your vision is clear. Stand firm and never give up. Be willing to make sacrifices. Enjoy the victory that comes with the organization, making sure they also have what they need. Communication is so important that if you don't know the language as a leader, you have to learn it.

People who you need to win

1. People with competitive edge who like to win

2. People who risk become their second nature

3. People who are ready to invest their whole life

4. People who are willing to pass the ball

5. People who not only want to win but also help others to win.

6. People who are creative and innovative.

Be on top of the game

1. Focus on your team and build them up

2. Prepare for crises and issues before they occur

3. Know your competitors and never underestimate them

4. Victory may come with affiliation and not with isolation

5. Learn from your mistakes and take advantage of adversity

6. Don't let setbacks cause you to lose the war—you may lose the battle but can still win the war

7. Enjoy your successes when it comes and then get back to work

Build up your momentum

1. When a problem is obvious, then go after it and resolve it

2. As a leader, you need to be motivated and a self-initiator

3. Accept responsibilities and deal with them, don't blame them on others

4. Focus on the issues with your team to find solutions

5. Don't allow issues to sidetrack you and your team

6. All staff should work with a unified attitude, checking tempers and egos

7. Develop a plan and communicate it with confidence

8. Have confidence in your plans before they leave your lips

What kills momentum?

a. Procrastination: Actions are the launching pad for your momentum but procrastination kills momentum. If there is a job to be done, don't wait but do it now.

b. Small victory: It doesn't matter if it is small victory, get on with it for the bigger one to come.

c. Your past: Focus on the positive and the future not on the past. Time lost shall not be regained, so why do you concentrate on the past. Know where you are going and go with full steam ahead not looking back. Be careful with the baggage of the past for it will hold your back.

d. Double mindedness: Come out of double mindedness for that would decrease your momentum. Deliver wherever necessary. If you are going to be doing something important, it is worth doing it now.

Passionate leaders

1. Passionate leaders go the extra mile because their heart is invested. People will buy into your heart and not your mind.

2. Cultivate a strong relationship so that people will sense that they are in it together.

3. Bring people to a social gathering to build up your team giving them a sense of belonging.

4. Conflict must be resolved quickly and in a mature way.

5. Keep your eyes open and continue to look for new and an innovative way to do things.

6. A passionate leader should always know why things happen and should be ready to give answers about them.

7. Passionate leaders find the movers, makers, and shakers who get the job done and multiply their efforts by investing in their lives.

8. Passionate leaders always avoid momentum fakers, takers, and breakers in all his dealings.

9. Passionate leaders know that momentum is not to be taken for granted since it doesn't last forever. Ride with it as long as it lasts.

Chapter 11

Living in the Past

Men have the tendency of dwelling in the past. For most of us our past seems to dictate everything that we do, both in the present and also the future. What was good in your past that you always want to go back to? What past glory can you bring to your present to enhance your future? How many of us remain on the ground when we fall and never rise, shake off the dust, and move on?

People tend to remain standstill when they lose their father, mother, brother, sister, uncle, aunt, friend, wife, or husband who was supporting them. Why do we allow the loss of a love one cripple us in our life, dwelling on the loss to hinder our progress? Our future does not depend on anyone but ourselves. Like Israel on the wilderness, we tend to depend on our past rather than what is available to work with for the future. When Moses the man of God died, the whole congregation of Israel kept mourning him for several days. They came to a standstill in their journey to the promised land. They lost focus on their God given dream. All hope and courage was gone. There was no desire in any of them to live but to wait for death to come. They surely murmured and complained about leaving Egypt and desired to go back. To these men and women, living was hell. They were in slavery in Egypt before Moses showed up to deliver them from the disastrous hand of Pharaoh and his gods. Yet they desired to go back Egypt.

Yes, they watched Moses perform all kind of miracles to prove to Pharaoh that God was in control and that God had sent him. They also witnessed the greatest miracle of all time by opening the Red Sea for Israel to walk through, but when the Egyptians tried to pass through, they drowned. This was not the end, but when they journeyed from the Red sea through the wilderness they saw many signs and miracles of Moses. In times of need they were assured that their God given promise was still in place. When they were in need of water, Moses struck the rock and water came for them to drink. When they needed food, Moses gave them manna and meat. When they sinned and God sent serpents among them, it was the same Moses who rose up the brazen serpent in the wilderness that whoever looks up to it was healed. Throughout their journey all their needs were met, any time they addressed them to Moses.

Who among them could replace Moses in the lives of Israel? They all realized that Moses was irreplaceable. Israel mourned like there was no tomorrow. It was here that God realized Israel's predicament. He intervened and appeared to Joshua the son of Nun, saying that his servant Moses was dead and that he should arise and take the people of Israel to cross over the River Jordan and that any place the sole of his feet shall tread He will give it to him. He promised to be with him just as had been with Moses.

Whenever I read through these Scriptures, I begin to wonder why God has to remind Joshua that his servant Moses was dead. Yes, they all knew that Moses was dead but to remind them again was uncalled for. God was telling Israel that there was no need to abandon the vision but to move on to take the land

He had promised. He was telling them not to allow their past to stop them from taking what belonged to them. They didn't need to give up on themselves. Since God was their source, life must go on. We can only stop living when our source goes dry. If God is our source, then we will never go dry. All his promises are "yes" and "amen" by us. When we press on, he would see us through. When we remain strong and of good courage, we will not be hindered. Yes, in the course of our journey we would be intimidated and face many obstacles and difficulties, but when we remain strong and of good courage we would prosper and have good success. When Joshua remained strong and courageous, he led Israel to the promise land.

The need to forget the past is necessary in our lives in order to enable us to move to our destination. Rahab did not consider her past as a prostitute but as someone who saved the spies sent by Joshua from death by hiding them. So also Ruth, a Moabite who grew up worshipping idols, did not have a promising start, but after turning to serve the true and only living God of Israel, she became part of the ancestry of King David and our Lord and Saviour Jesus Christ.

Whoever thought that Zacchaeus could be a follower of our Lord Jesus overnight, considering his situation as an embezzler and an enemy to true justice? But when he put his past behind him and received Jesus, he was saved and became a philanthropist. The Lord put it very nicely that there are twelve hours in a day. My last twelve hours should not hinder me from achieving what I want to achieve today or tomorrow.

We can surely not talk about the principles of the past without touching on what and how Paul treated his past. Philippians 3: 13-14 reads, "Brethren I do not count myself to have apprehended but one thing I do, forgetting those things which are behind and reaching forward to those things which are ahead. I press toward the goal for the prize of the upward call of God in Christ Jesus"

To understand these Scriptures we need to know Paul's past, which in this passage he intended to forget. He said if anyone was to have confidence in the flesh, He the more. He was circumcised the eighth day from the stock of Israel, of the tribe of Benjamin, a Hebrew of Hebrews and concerning the law a Pharisee and concerning the righteousness which is in the law blameless. He said, but what things were gain to me these I have counted loss for Christ (Philippians 3: 3-7 paraphrased)

Paul counted all the above as rubbish that he might gain Christ. Remember, gaining the excellence of the knowledge of Christ Jesus was Paul's ultimate goal and that anything short of this was considered as rubbish. If he depended on the past glory or failure, Paul realized that he will never get to his destination.

If your future or your vision is very important to you, then be like Paul and forget about the past and press on the mark to win the prize. The winning athlete crossing the finish line should be your focus. It is not the cheering crowd or the falling athlete next to your lane but the tape on the finish line. Paul said this is the pattern for us. Your past and my past should not hinder us to reach our God given goals.

Remember, it takes those who would be strong and courageous, pressing forward the mark of the upward call, to win or succeed in life. We should always be marching on. If we stand still we deprive ourselves of our God given substance. If you are bed stricken, begin to sit up; if you are sitting up, try to stand; if you are standing, begin to walk; if you are walking, begin to run; if you are running, begin to fly. Nothing ventured, nothing gained. If you want to get somewhere, you need to arise and go. Never say that is my end or I can't, but rise and shine. Grease your elbow and strengthen your feeble legs for the vision is for an appointed time though it may tarry, it shall surely come to pass. The business can be successful if you put your mind to it. You cannot be good at everything all the time, but don't give up when you try and fail. Tackling new ventures usually means learning by trial and error. A persistent end speaks for itself. Do you want to get somewhere? Then arise and press on the mark and go.

Chapter 12

Make Use of Your Gifts

There is always the likelihood of sweeping our gifts under the carpet without even realizing it. Each and every one of us has a gift, but the way we use our gift will make the difference. When we are determined and persist in working with our gifts, we will surely become successful. It doesn't matter how big or small we are. Size and colour don't make any difference—your determination does.

The book of Proverbs will help us to understand the how important to make use of our gifts. Proverbs 30: 24 reads; "There are four things which are little upon the earth, but they are exceeding wise."

One of these little things is the ant. Let us for a moment look at the lifestyle of the ant. In the next verse of the same chapter of Proverbs we read, "The ants are a people not strong yet they prepare their meat in the summer."

Ants are little creatures but use their strength wisely to store up food and prepare for the future.

We may also not be strong as others, but if we will arise and use our strength wisely as they do, we will get somewhere. How many times do we even make use of the lands around our environment and homes? Ants don't think only about now but also the future. So also can we with proper preparation be able to take care of our future without many problems. We are living in a day and age where saving for the rainy days is more important than ever.

Ants live in colonies and draw resources from each other, dividing the task at hand among themselves with builders, workers, soldiers, and bearers distributing the tasks at hand among themselves. Each and every member of the group is very important, and they need each other. People should always realize that each and every one of us is important when it comes to achieving our aims in the life. When resources are shared, there will always be enough for everyone and there will be leftovers.

The male ants have wings by which they fly, but they have short lives. Those who seek to outrun their fellows to become better run to their death. When we stick together we will live. Amos 2: 2 says, "Can two walk together, except they agreed?" Also Matthew 18: 19 says, "Again I say unto you, that if two of you shall agree on earth as touching anything that they shall ask, it shall be done for them of my Father which is in heaven".

To succeed we need to stick together, work together, share together, and store for the future. This is the life of a wise man.

Ants with so little strength are able to store food for the future. These harvester ants are found in regions of relative food shortage and therefore, dependent on the diet seeds. Most ants maintain underground colonies that like bees work on the division of labour principle. Whilst some attend to the cultivation of fungi, others milk the aphids for the secreted hand dew. The soldier ants also guide the colony. Most ants are wingless, sterile workers, but they live longer.

Solomon compared a sluggard to be opposite of an ant. A sluggard is one who loves his ease, sticks to nothing, minds no business, lives in idleness, brings nothing to pass, cannot accomplish anything good, and is careless in all manner of business. He's slothful as his sure way to poverty.

A sluggard needs instructions to help him observe the ant, being an inferior creature but able to accomplish so much. These instructions will bring the sluggard not to consider its own weakness but to learn the good and the best for the ant. If we are to imitate others in that which is good, we must consider their ways. If we diligently observe what they do, we may do likewise. Learn wisdom, consider, and be wise. Our desire in learning is not only to know, but also to be wise. We learn to provide for ourselves in the future not only here and now. Not to eat up all but in gathering time treasure up for a spending time. We must take pain and labour in our business. They may labour under inconveniences, but come summer when others are having fun, the ant will be busy gathering its food. Ants help each other. It is our wisdom to improve the season whilst that favours us, because that may be done, that which cannot be done at all, or not well done at another time. Whilst there is enough light we should strive to walk. Come darkness we may never be able to move at all. Make use of both your time and strength whilst you have it.

Let look at the second little thing the Bible says it is wise. It is the conies. Proverbs 30: 26 says; "The conies are but a feeble folk, yet make their houses in the rocks".

With their feebleness and the importance of security they make their homes secure in rocks. If conies depend on strongholds for their homes and security, what more do Christians need to have than Jesus Christ as our rock, since we cannot do it with our own strength? He was the rock that followed Israel in their wilderness journey. Jesus is the rock from which Israel drunk from when they became thirsty. Christ is a believer's strong foundation on which we depend on. Don't forget the rock followed Israel in their wilderness journey from Egypt to Canaan.

Conies contend with the wild goats on the mountains but still survive. If God be for us, who can be against us? (Romans 8: 31) They that have no might God increases their strength (Isaiah 40: 29-31). When we make use of the little strength that we have we will surely get to our destination. We should always remember that size is no excuse if we want to go somewhere. It is not what you are but who you are. Make sure Christ is your rock.

The third little thing is nothing but the locust. Proverbs 30: 27 reads; "The locust have no king, yet go they forth all of them by bands".

Locusts are small but can bring down a kingdom. Together locusts are very destructive. They are also unstoppable and can devour a whole land of its vegetation. Remember they are bold and never give up. They will use every means to get to their destination. If they can't get through the door, they come through the window. If not through the window, they come through the gutter. If not through the gutter, they will come through the porch. One thing they don't do is give up. How many times do we give up and quit as believers when situation don't work the way we want it?

They unite and operate in bands that become unstoppable. Remember, one can chase a thousand and two can chase ten thousand (Deut. 32: 30). A strong team can achieve more than several individuals working separately.

Locust can't fly very much, but they wait for the wind direction to fly. We should move when God moves our direction. We should remain sensitive to the wind of God, which is the Holy Spirit. When we are led by the Spirit, we shall not fulfil the desires of the flesh. If we want to experience the supernatural, then we need to move with the Spirit of the Lord. When the Spirit of the Lord came upon the prophets, kings, and the priests, they were able to do more. Christians today have the Holy Spirit living big inside of us. We therefore need to arise and do what we have been called to do without hindrance.

Locusts have no king, yet they move in a band. If we sit and fold our arms the right time will never come, but if you move, God will surely direct you. In Joshua 1:11 Israel has to move to take possession of the land the Lord their God has given them. Remember, it did not come on a silver platter. They had to go for it. Yes, God gave Israel manna to eat in the wilderness, but they were to arise every morning to collect it. They were to come home with it and prepare it before they could eat it. God is seeking those men and women who are ready to say "Lord here I am send me" (Isaiah 6: 8). Are you ready to be send? Deuteronomy 28: 13 says when we move we will be the head and not the tail; above not beneath.

Locusts do not use their wings as an excuse not to fly. If you can't fly, you can hop; if you can't hop, you can run; if you can't run, you can walk; if you can't walk, you can crawl. Just do something and be useful. Never say I can't.

The last but not the least little thing in Proverbs is the spider. Proverb 30: 28 says, "The spider take hold with her hands, and is in king's palaces".

Spiders have everything necessary to survive and succeed. You destroy a spider's web now, and in a few hours a new one is in place. 2 Peter 1: 3-4 says, "God's divine power has given unto us all things that pertain unto life and godliness through the knowledge of him that has called us to glory and virtue". Your future does not depend on nor is it determined by who you know and who you don't know. The power to fulfil your destiny is within you. When God made us, we were good. That alone is enough.

2 Timothy 1: 6 says stir up the gift of God in you. You may be down, but you are not out. What is at work within you is greater than what is at work around you. As long as you have what God put within you, you have got it. When the smoke clears, you must rise up in faith and build.

How can a spider walk across the sticky threads of its web and not get stuck? It is because of the oil its feet prevents him for being bogged down. One of the reasons why we need to be filled with the Holy Ghost is for us to be able to go where we want to go and not be blocked or intimidated. Psalm 92: 10 says, "We need to be anointed with fresh oil".

Spiders have eight eyes, but they barely see with them. They hunt with the help of the four follicles on their legs, which are full of sensitivity and can discern what goes around the spider. 1 John 2: 20 declares that we will know things. Why? It is because the Holy Spirit lives inside of us to direct us. John 16: 13 says, we cannot explain it; it is the anointing that breaks the yolk and teaches us all things.

Some spiders have much venom in them to kill anything that comes in contact with them. When we release what is within us, it brings us miracles. What we give out is either faith or fear. Proverbs 18: 21 says, "Life and death is in the power of the tongue". Open your mouth and declare it. It is written and it shall come to pass. Matthew 4: 11 says when you are under attack, open your mouth and your angels would minister unto you.

Always remember, size doesn't determine your potential, your spirit does. No matter where you start, you can make it up to the kings' palace. Keep producing, and you will get to your destination. Psalm 92: 14 says, "We should bring forth fruits in old age".

Don't sit down if you're old and count your wrinkles, get up and dress even if you are not going anywhere. If you can't fly, get in a car. If you can't get in a car, run. If you can't run, walk. If you can't walk, creep. If you can't creep, stand up. Don't just stay where you are. If you're lying down, sit up. If you can't sit up, wriggle your toes, your fingers, your head, your neck, and your body. Just do something. Don't let the Devil bring you down or run you out of the game. Keep producing just as the spider does.

The power that is in you can either break you or build you.

Chapter 13

The End Shall Be Great

Do you have the desire to be great? I do. I have the desire to be great and even grow greater. My end is determined daily by the very seed that I sow. I do not allow myself to be bogged down by anything that comes my way. Neither am I intimidated by the negative attacker that always tries to show up when he is not wanted. The race is set, the vision is known, and the dream needs to be fulfilled. No one runs the race for me; neither do I wait for someone to do the training for me, since I alone need to run that race. I choose my race and train to get myself approved and then ultimately win. My ability to listen, my desire to win and to share, my understanding of the vision, and my determination to pursue the dream will bring the victory I desire. When I am in the will of God and ready to do the things that he has called me to do, then victory is always guaranteed.

When everything that surrounds me becomes like shadows I know my God given vision would always prevail. When I fall and my face is in the mud, damp, lonely, destitute, and despairing, there is only one thing that I know, and that is the righteous man shall fall seven times but the Lord shall raise him up. I may be down but not out. I only need to pick myself up and clear the mud and move on. I may find myself in a tunnel with darkness all around me, but at the end of the tunnel there is light that awaits me. I may be sick but not dead. I know perfectly well that I shall not die but live to declare the works of the Lord. The Lord has so much in store for me, so I always make myself available for him to show himself mighty in me. My finances may be in shambles, but I know that the Lord became poor that I may be rich. With Christ on my side, my resources would never dry up. I have come to realize that it is no longer I who live but Christ if I am crucified with Christ. Every life that I live, I live by faith in Christ Jesus who loves me and gave himself for me. I can because Christ can; therefore, my success is guaranteed.

Over the years, I have come to realize that the greatest weapon that the Devil wants from my life is my faith. But if my faith in the Lord Jesus is in shape, then the enemy would always be a defeated foe. If my faith is touched, then I would be defeated.

Faith in action

Many people strongly believe that some pastors prosper because God favours them more. That can't be true. Yes, God may love them and may be answering their prayers more than others, but we need to understand that God shows no favouritism. He loves us and has given each one of us a measure of faith. We can choose to do something about our faith or hide it under the carpet. It is our choice. Your success depends on it. If it is faith then do something about it. Don't just sit down and expect miracles to fall on your bosom. It is not going to happen. If you are expecting a miracle, then let your faith do it.

We all agree that God gave Israel manna on the desert but they had to wake up every morning to pick it up. The manna did not just fall on their plates. They needed to have faith that God would make it available every morning. They also needed to strengthen themselves to walk the fields to pick them up. When they come home they had to prepare it to their own taste before they could enjoy it. Those who did stayed at home and expected to be fed went through the day without food.

I have repeated the manna issue because I need you to understand that whatever situation you may find yourself in, it is only you who can change it. James put it very nicely that "faith without work is dead". Do something with what you believe. If you are expecting to get somewhere the only thing you have to do is rise up and go. Do you want to be somebody? Then start now to be that someone. I can't change your life, but I can only help to guide you in the ways that would be beneficial to you if you heed.

Paul put it very nicely in 2 Corinthians 1: 20 that "for all the promises of God are yes and in Him Amen, to the glory of God through us". Yes many are the blessings of God that he has promised us in his word, but it is the believer who has to implement them in his life. The promises are given to you, and you can either take them or leave them. No hurt feelings—It is your choice. Those who choose it choose life for themselves, but those who ignore it, suffer the effects. No one is in any position to change your vision or dream. That authority is in your own hands.

The Israelites after the death of Moses in the desert thought that was the end of their journey to the promised land, until God called out Joshua to arise and take the children of Israel across the Jordan into the promised land. We, like Israel, are always waiting for someone to tell us what to do. Yes, we believe God can do it, but we never expect God to do it through us. We are always looking up to someone else to do it. We need to arise and run the race that is set before us with fear and trembling.

Paul said we should fight the good fight of faith. Believers are at war, but with our faith intact, victory shall always be ours.

There are many men and women of faith in the Bible that we need to learn from. With their faith they touched the realm of the miraculous. They were able to reach out to the supernatural. When we look at men and women like Abraham, Moses, David, Daniel, Elijah, Mary, and Rahab to name a few, we will see the importance of faith. They conquered and subdued kingdoms. They were life changers. There were fire starters, rain and water makers. They were battle winners, operating against the odds, who took God at his word and worked miracles. Remember, you are no different.

Elijah prayed for rain in 1 Kings 18: 41-46:

> Then Elijah said to Ahab, go up, eat and drink for there is the sound of abundance of rain. So Ahab went up to eat and drink. And Elijah went up to the top of Carmel, then he bowed down to the ground, and put his face between his knees, and said to his servant, "go up now, look toward the sea". So he went up and looked, and said, There is nothing, And seven times he said, "Go again" Then it came to pass the seventh time, that he said "There is a cloud, as small as a man's hand, rising out of the sea". So he said "Go up and say to Ahab Prepare your chariot, and go down before the rain stops you". Now it happened in the meantime that the sky became black with clouds and wind and there was a heavy rain. So Ahab rode away and went to Jezreel. Then the hand of the Lord came upon Elijah, and he

girded up his loins and ran ahead of Ahab to the
entrance of Jezreel

This was the time that, because of the sins of the people, Elijah
the Tishbite from the inhabitants of Gilead prophesied that
there would be no rain on the land for three and half years
according to his word. Who was this Elijah anyway? The
scripture indicates that he was a Tishbite, a desert dweller.
Come to think of it, what good can come out of the desert? Is
it not scorpions, snakes, dry and scorching heat during the day,
and the chilling cold of the clear sky night? In the eyes of men,
Elijah was Mr Nobody, but he allowed faith to arise in him that
life and death is in the power of the tongue and they that love it
shall eat the good there of. Miraculously, there was no rain for
three and half years on the land. When the people turned away
from their sins and returned to trust the living God, he prayed
again and rain came forth.

Verse 41 of this chapter says Elijah said to Ahab the King, go
up, eat, and drink, for there is the sound of abundance rain.
Ahab trusted the words of Elijah even though the skies were
clear with no cloud cover. If this man has been able to stop the
skies from giving rain, then he can equally request the skies to
give again. So, Ahab went up eat and drink. If it was you and
I, we would sit and wait for the rain, but not so with Elijah. He
knew that the vision comes to pass with much business. So,
he went on top of Mount Carmel and prayed for the rain. He
persisted in his prayer until the rains came. Just as he requested,
it did happen as if it was a light thing to request. Our faith in
action will always yield the results. Not only did he receive
rain, but also the power of God came over him in such a way
that he out run the chariots of Ahab to the entrance of Jezreel.

Fire from Heaven

Don't forget it was the same person who prayed for fire from heaven to burn the bullock on the altar. This happened when faith arose in him to prepare the altar of God that had been broken by the king and the people because of sin. Israel turned its back on God, their covenant partner, to serve Baal. Therefore, Elijah challenged the people to choose between God and Baal. He requested two bullocks to be given between the prophets of Baal and himself. The bullock was to be prepared and placed on an altar without fire. The challenge was that the god who answered by fire he would be their god.

The prophets of Baal took the bullock and prepared it first, and called the name of their god from morning till noon, but there was no voice. Elijah insisted they should cry louder, for their god may be meditating, busy, on a journey, or sleeping and must be awakened. The scriptures indicate that they cried aloud and cut themselves as was their custom with knives and lances until blood came, but there was no voice even until the evening.

It was at this time that Elijah also called the people to himself to witness what God was about to do in their midst. The time for evening sacrifice was God ordained. It was the time for the people of Israel to come before him with their sacrifice and also to worship him. Israel had forsaken this very commandment for some time. This law of their covenant God had been neglected. Elijah therefore wanted the fear of God to be before the people that they may not sin against Him. To him, it was a big test for the people to have the fear of God.

He therefore prepared the altar which was broken in the name of the Lord. He chopped the bullock into pieces and placed it on the altar. He made a trench around the altar and then requested it to be filled with water. This was done three times. That was a very strange thing to do under normal circumstances. If I want to burn something why do I need to cover it with water before setting it on fire? Elijah surely wanted all to know that this was not under his own control but God's. He therefore prayed to God that He was the only God, and that He should also turn the people's heart back again. After this prayer, the scriptures say the fire of the Lord came down and consumed the burnt sacrifice and the wood and the stones and the dust and also licked up the water that was in the trench.

When the people saw this they fell on their faces and said "The Lord, He is God". What brought about this? It was the faith of someone, an ordinary man who knew what God can do when we serve and call upon his name. Remember, God's power is in you. He is always waiting on you to do something about the situation so He can honour himself. When you are blessed it brings glory and honour to God.

Isaac stands for faith (Genesis 26: 1-12)

It is always easy to take faith for granted. This usually happens because we mix faith with belief. When we talk of belief it means to accept as true or real. It also means to think, assume, or to suppose. This is different from faith. Faith is a strong belief in something without proof—complete confidence or trust in a person or remedy without concrete evidence. The Scriptures say faith is "the substance of things hoped for, the evidence of thing not seen". It means actually having the trust in something without any proof. It is this faith that we need in the Kingdom of God. We are Kingdom people, therefore we need to apply the Kingdom principles. Just as a doctor works with the medicinal principles in order to bring healing to the sick, and the natural man the natural principles of this world, so is every believer in the Kingdom of God. If you operate outside the principles of the Kingdom laid down in the word of God, the Bible, you will fall flat on your face. The scriptures work, but for those who are in the Kingdom.

One man that used the principles to his advantage was Isaac the son of Abraham. There was famine in the land, and the Lord appeared to Isaac and asked him not to go to Egypt, being the most likely thing to do, but stay in Gerar and he will be with him and bless him. This was not an easy thing to do, living without food because of famine. There were other lands or places that one could seek food and accommodation in order to survive. Why stay in one place and die?

The Scriptures indicate that Isaac obeyed and stayed on the land of Gerar as God has commanded him. But then he didn't just stay and wait for a miracle of abundance to come his way. The Scriptures say that Isaac sowed on the land and reaped in the same year a hundredfold and the Lord blessed him. They continue to say that the man began to prosper and continued to prosper until he became very prosperous. He had so many possessions of flock and possessions of herds and a great number of servants that the Philistines envied him. What a wealth!

One today may wonder why we say Isaac became prosperous having sheep and cattle and servants. In those days a man's worth was measured by the number of slaves or servants, sheep, and cattle that they had. Isaac's simple faith in the Lord brought about his worth. The chances that Isaac had are equally open to us.

The Scriptures say in the book of Isaiah the first chapter that if we are willing and obedient we shall eat the good of the land. The good things of the Kingdom of God belong to all. We need to let faith arise in us to take them. They will not fall in our laps if we just sit and fold our aims. We have to arise and shine. Like Isaac, we have to move in line with what the Lord has promised. Yes, the promise is for an appointed time, and it will surely come to pass. There are no ifs and buts in the promise. When we do the promise, the blessings would come. If you are willing, then arise and do something, for the victory is to follow.

Don't look at your circumstances and the people who are dying because of the current situation, or the people who are out of business because of the recession. Your dreams and visions are different from others. Remember that your calling and destination are equally different from everyone else. You need to concentrate on your God given instruction, and victory shall always be yours and even overtake you.

Paul's missionary journey (Acts 27: 1-44)

Paul in the course of his ministry was arrested. He appeared before King Agrippa who found no fault with Paul and might have set him free had he not appealed to Caesar. Paul therefore had to be sent to Rome to appeal before Caesar. It was on this journey that Paul encountered so many difficulties, but his faith remained intact.

To appear before Caesar, Paul was delivered with other prisoner to a centurion named Julius. When they got to Sidon, Julius treated Paul very well and even gave him liberty to go to his friends to receive care. When they took off and sailed to Myra, a city if Lycia, the centurion found a ship which was sailing to Italy. They encountered many difficulties with the wind against them. Having spent much time and sailing becoming now dangerous, Paul advised them that the voyage will end in a disaster and much loss for both the ship, cargo, and also for lives. The funny thing was that his advice was not taken on board.

They kept sailing, and later were deceived by the south wind that blew softly, supposing that they had obtained their desire. But when the tempestuous head wind arose, the ship was caught and could not head into the wind. So they let her drive, and later secured the skiff with difficulties. Fearing they might run aground on the Syrtis Sands, they struck sail and were so driven. Because they were so tempest-tossed, the next day they lightened the ship and threw the ship's tackle overboard with their own hands. For many days, they did not see the sun or stars. They lost hope and gave up even eating.

After many days of fasting, Paul urged them to take heart for there would be no loss of life among them except for loss of the ship. The angel of the Lord had urged him not to be afraid, because he will be brought before Caesar. Paul also said to them that he believed God that it would be just as he has been told. He also assured them that it will come with difficulties. For fourteen nights they were driven up and down the Adriatic Sea but later sensed they were closer to land. They took some soundings, and fearing they might run aground they dropped four anchors from the stern and prayed for day to come. Here the sailors were seeking to escape from the ship, but Paul said unless they stayed on the ship they would not be saved. Then the soldiers cut away the ropes of the skiff and let it fall off.

As day was about to dawn, Paul implored them all to take food for nourishment for their survival. Paul therefore took bread and gave thanks to God in their presence and began to eat. They also encouraged themselves and ate. After eating, they lightened the ship by throwing the wheat into the sea. Having spotted a beach, they let go the anchors into the sea, and losing rudder ropes they hoisted the mainsail to the wind and made it to the shore, but struck a place where two seas met they ran the ship aground and remained immovable. The stern was broken by the violence waves.

The soldiers planned to kill the prisoners, but the centurion intervened wanting to save Paul. The centurion requested that those who could swim should jump overboard. The rest lay on some on boards and others on the parts of the ship and escaped to safety on land. All the two hundred and seventy six persons were saved.

The question is how did it happen? The sea could have easily consumed them. The soldiers could have also carried on their evil plans of mass killing. It was all due to Paul's persistent faith. He trusted God, knowing that the God who had promised them safety was able to see them through.

It is not your circumstances but what God is saying or has said. He is able to carry His promises through, and nothing can hinder him. In business, you can equally encounter storms and evil winds and men to challenge your faith, but you should always allow faith to arise in you. The God who has called you is able to fulfil what he has promised.

Whatever your situation, if you put your mind to it and trust God, it will surely come to pass. The storm, the wind, and the evil plans are no match to the promise made by God. They will only come to intimidate and derail you. But remember, if it is faith then do it, for it will come to pass.

Chapter 14

It Is Finished

It is one thing trying to fight your own battle, but it is another to know someone has fought it for you and that you are only there to celebrate the victory. Believe victory is a result of what Christ has done and not what we fought for ourselves. If Christ did it for me, then what do I need to do again than to walk in that victory? Paul says in Christ Jesus we are more than conquerors. Yes, we haven't been to war yet, but Christ has. He took your place and my place and then handed victory to us. It is only those who are in him who see and enjoy this victory. If you are in Christ, then you need to realize that there is victory that has been accomplished for you.

Collins English Dictionary defines success as the favourable outcome of something attempted. It can also be said to be the attainment of wealth or fame. We say someone is successful when the person accomplishes his aim in the manner he desire. I view success as accomplishing all aims and desires in any giving situation. This really means that, if a favourable outcome is going to be achieved, then I need to work at it. I cannot just sit and expect things to come to pass. If I am ever going to get somewhere in life, than I need to arise and go. It's nothing ventured, nothing gained in this world. Since Christ has won the victory for me, then I need to make sure I identify myself with his finished work to see the victory in my life. My victory is as a result of his death and resurrection.

There should be a balance in my success. If I am going to be successful in finances, then I have to be successful also in my health. Physically, financially, spiritually, and materially I have to see success all round. Why do I have to see it only financially to the detriment of my spiritual success? It should be success all round, and that is God's way. It doesn't really make much difference—it is either you are successful or you are not. It comes to those who seek it, desire it, and work for it. You may ask, can I have it when I seek it? Yes, you can. Desire it and work for it believing in oneself. It is something that you need to attempt. It is you who will make it happen. Make use of your God given ability or talents, with the measure of faith that you have been bestirred with. If you seek it, you will surely find it. We have been living on the fences, waiting for God to act or do something in our life. Whilst God is waiting to accomplish His purposes in our life, we are asking ourselves when he will intervene in our circumstances. The will of God needs to be seen in our life for us to be fulfilled. The book Ezekiel will help you to understand the will of God for your life.

Ezekiel 37: 1-14 says:

> The hand of the LORD was upon me, and carried me out in the Spirit of the Lord and set me down in the mist of the valley which was full of bones, And caused me to pass by them round about: and, behold, there were very many in the open valley; and, lo, they were very dry. And he said unto me, Son of man, can these bones live? And I answered, O Lord GOD, thou knowest. Again he said unto me, Prophesy upon these bones, and

say unto them, O ye dry bones, hear the word of the LORD. Thus saith the Lord GOD unto these bones; Behold, I will cause breath to enter into you, and ye shall live: And I will lay sinews upon you, and will bring up flesh upon you, and cover you with skin, and put breath in you, and ye shall live; and ye shall know that I am the LORD. So I prophesied as I was commanded: and as I prophesied, there was a noise, and behold a shaking, and the bones came together, bone to his bone. And when I beheld, lo, the sinews and the flesh came up upon them, and the skin covered them above: but there was no breath in them. Then said he unto me, Prophesy unto the wind, prophesy, son of man, and say to the wind, Thus saith the Lord GOD; Come from the four winds, O breath, and breathe upon these slain, that they may live. So I prophesied as he commanded me, and the breath came into them, and they lived, and stood up upon their feet, an exceeding great army.

Then he said unto me, Son of man, these bones are the whole house of Israel: behold, they say, Our bones are dried, and our hope is lost: we are cut off for our parts. Therefore prophesy and say unto them, Thus saith the Lord GOD; Behold, O my people, I will open your graves, and cause you to come up out of your graves, and bring you into the land of Israel. And ye shall know that I am the LORD, when I have opened your graves, O my people, and brought you up out of your graves, And shall put my spirit in you, and ye shall live, and I shall place you in your own land:

then shall ye know that I the LORD have spoken
it, and performed it, saith the LORD. (KJV)

This story is an indication of how God does not override our
will, but always seeks our will and desire in the situations that
we come across and that also confront us. Our future and our
destiny are always in our own hands. God always seeks an
avenue in our lives to work with us. Just as Scriptures indicate
that the Holy Spirit is our helper. He comes to help if we ask
Him, but He does not come and do the work for us. When you
seek assistance, you will call for someone, yes! And when the
person comes, he comes to assist but not to do the whole work
for you. God comes in to help when we pray for his help.

Yes! Our situation can be very dry as that of Ezekiel, but God
would be waiting on us to call for help. He will be waiting
for you and me to speak to the situation. Life and death is in
the power of the tongue, but it is they that love it that eat the
fruit of it. If you want to change the situation in your life, do it
through your tongue.

Let's look at the question the Lord put before the prophet
Ezekiel in the valley of the dry bones: "Son of man can these
bones live?" It was not an easy question which demanded an
answer. It was similar to the many questions that confront
believers every day of their lives.

Ezekiel placed complete faith in God. It is God alone who
knows all things that pertain to this life. Scriptures indicate that
secret things belong to God. And the same Scriptures continue
to say that "but it has been revealed to his people. If you are a
believer that means you are also part of the people of God. That
means the answers to the secrets of this life are within reach to
you."

For the perfect will of God to come to pass, Ezekiel had to trust the word of God and do just as commanded. Like Ezekiel, can you put your total trust in God and expect Him to come to your aid.

Verses 4 and 8 say God works step by step and does not skip a gradient. If we are going to work with God, we must as well follow his lead. Let's for a second look at how God worked with Ezekiel to bring to pass the answers to his situation.

Ezekiel had to speak so:

1. Bones come together

2. Sinews to come on the bone

3. Flesh to come upon the sinews

4. Skin to cover the flesh

5. Breath to enter the body so they can live.

These were specific instructions given to Ezekiel to command. It is by faith that we call things that are not, as though they were. It was Ezekiel who had to speak to the bones, the sinews, the flesh, the skin, and the four breaths to come. We may think it is God who has to do the commanding and the speaking, but that is not the case. We are called by Isaiah to come and reason together with God no matter our circumstances.

One thing that I realized is that, when Ezekiel spoke as commanded, nature heard and responded. We have power over nature. It our God given right and no one takes it away from us. The Devil tried it in the garden when Adam and Eve sold out to him, but through the resurrected Christ we have that power and authority back.

Remember, the breath is of God but not of man. Man is dead if he has not the breath of God. There is also the tendency for man to forget God. When Ezekiel commanded the bones, the sinews, the flesh, and the skin there were all the signs that he could do it without God, until he realized that there was no breath in the dead bodies. He had called them to being. He had to go back to God for fresh instruction and anointing to carry on the next stage of his creation.

We sometimes forget that it is God who enables us to do more and exceedingly. We want to go solo until we fall flat on our face. David cried to the Lord take not your Holy Ghost from me and restore to me the joy of your salvation. We constantly need the Spirit direction. There is always the need to call upon God for directions.

We need to have the tendency of going back to God for perfect direction.

God said to Abraham "walk before me and be thou perfect". Perfection comes to those who walk with God every day of their lives.

Ezekiel went back to the dead bodies. God who is rich in mercy and giver of life also directed him with the next point of his quest of causing life to come to the dry bones. Remember, in our hopeless situations we need to ask God for further directions as to what to do to bring life into our lives. The situation could be as bad as death itself, but if we go back to God for directions, he will surely show us the way. There is nothing under the sun which is not within his control. But He doesn't get involved until we, his servants, ask Him to. He is the master planner, and there is nothing too hard for him. The moment we give up or think we can do it without him, that will be the beginning of our fall. There is always the need to build a stronger relationship with God. Accept the invitation to reason with him, and the good of the land shall be yours. How? because the Lord will direct you, and open the doors to you.

There is no part-time relationship with God. Dry bones indicate it is the Devil that comes to steal, kill, and to destroy, but Christ came that we might have life and have it in abundance. He is able to restore the years the enemy has destroyed. When we yield our lives to the architect of the miraculous, then all things will work together for our good. Christ said if He be lifted up, he will draw all men to himself. When we realize our role and God's role, we will always win and see the glory of God. It is only with God that we win. For winning ways seek God, and he will direct you in the things to do. When we talk about prophecy, we are referring to saying what God's word says and agreeing with it.

Matthew helps us to understand the benefit of the death of Christ on the cross. Matthew 27: 50-54 says:

> Jesus, when he had cried again with a loud voice, yielded up the ghost. And, behold, the veil of the temple was rent in twain from the top to the bottom; and the earth did quake, and the rocks rent; And the graves were opened; and many bodies of the saints which slept arose, And came out of the graves after his resurrection, and went into the holy city, and appeared unto many. Now when the centurion, and they that were with him, watching Jesus, saw the earthquake, and

those things that were done, they feared greatly, saying, Truly this was the Son of God. And many women were there beholding afar off, which followed Jesus from Galilee, ministering unto him: Among which was Mary Magdalene, and Mary the mother of James and Joseph, and the mother of Zebedee's children.

Matthew helps us to understand the finished work of the Lord at the cross. This is where he cried, "It is finished". Finished for what? It is finished for your trials, for your sickness, for your financial problems, and for your spiritual instability? Was it finished for your bareness, your pain, you addictions, your immoral acts, for your darkness and daily mourning and lack of faith—not to mention our sins and our iniquities? When he cried "It is finished," it was not a cry of despair, defeat, or exhaustion, but victory over the Devil who had stolen what belongs to the children of God. This is the purpose of his coming, and with this cry He declared his accomplishment.

John 19: 30 says, So when Jesus had received the sour wine, He said "it is finished!" And bowing down his head, He gave up his spirit.

"It is finished" was not a cry of despair, exhaustion, or defeat but a cry of victory. The purpose for which he came had been accomplished. It was the Lord Jesus who accomplished everything for you and me. He came that you and I may have life and have it in abundance. This life in abundance came to pass when he cried "It is finished".

John 20: 7 says t "The linen cloth and the handkerchief by itself indicated the finished work of the Lord. This handkerchief was meant to wipe away his sweat and tears. There was therefore no need for it if he had accomplished his work. He did not rush off but took his time to complete what he had started to do for mankind by folding away the handkerchief on the side."

Christ gave up his spirit. He dismissed his spirit by his own power. In death the Lord demonstrated his royal authority. No one took his life away from him, but he laid it down himself. Let he who reads understand that he lives, he moves, and has his being only in the finished work of our Lord and Saviour Jesus Christ. He cried with a loud voice and gave up his spirit. The Scriptures state that the earth quaked and the mountains rent, and there was thundering. Remember, nature respond when it hears the voice of the Lord.

Let's look at some of the things that happened through His death.

1. The curtains in the temple were torn in twain from top to bottom. This was the Lord opening new doors and ways for his children to have access to God. Whilst it was only the Jews who formerly had access to God, now the Gentiles could also come to the throne of grace to have mercy from God. We who were not a people are now sons of God. Paul says, if sons, then co-heirs with Christ. We have boldness and access to the presence of God with fear.

2. The earth quaking was an indication of the authority of the enemy shaken and his prisons bars broken. With the finished work of Christ any plans of the enemy against us are nullified, for his foundation has been shaken. The chains and shackles we were bound with have all been made loose. The Devil has no more hold on us. Paul

says in all these we are more than conquers. Truly we can, for we are able.

3. Rocks split declaring the stronghold of the enemy in shatters through the power of God when he raised Jesus from the death.

4. Graves were opened, indicating Christ destroying the power of death. No matter how many secret places the Devil hides us, the good Lord is able to bring us out.

In Mark 16: 7 the Lord declared to the woman to go to his disciples and Peter and tell them about the good news. This shows how the Lord delivers us in the hour of our despair. His banner over us is love. He does not even remember our sins and our trials and our denial. We need to wait for his love. Don't just run off like Judas. Peter was not left out of the good news and its blessings and neither should we. Christ is always ready to give us the second chance. Don't let sin stop you, for the Lord has not given up on you, so don't give up on yourself.

Paul helps us to understand the finished work of the Lord better. Colossian 2: 13-15 says:

> And you being dead in your trespasses and the uncircumcision of your flesh, he has made a live together with Him, having forgiven you all trespasses, having wiped out the handwriting of requirements that was against us, which was contrary to us. And He has taken it out of the way, having nailed it to the cross. Having disarmed principalities and powers, He made a public spectacle of them, triumphing over them in it.

Not only are our sins and iniquities forgiven on the cross, but also those ordinances that condemned us have also been removed by the death of Christ. The handwriting of the ordinance that was against us has been wiped out. The cross that was meant for Christ defeat turned out to be a victory for Christ. At the cross, Christ vanquished his foes, took away their weapons, and made a public spectacle of them. Believers today walk as soldiers, who are marching on the street showing off our victory by making a public spectacle of our enemies—not because of what we have done but because of what Jesus has accomplished for us.

Ephesians 4: 7 says, "But to each one of us grace was given according to the measure of Christ gift. Therefore He says; when he ascended on high he led captivity captive And He gave gifts to men". The fullness of Gods gifts flows through the believers abundantly. Through His death, not only do we have asses to Him, but He has also made gifts abound for us. Grace has been given to all who believe. This grace is the unmerited favour of God to us. Spiritual gifts have been given to all who believe in the finished work of God.

Remember, through his death, Christ translated us from the kingdom of darkness into his marvellous light. He turn our sickness into health, He became poor that you and I might be rich. He turned our death into life eternal. What more do we need since we live and have our being in Christ? There is nothing more that we can do except to embrace what the Lord has done for us and live by faith in them.

Chapter 15

Positive Ways to Grow Resources

Having realiz ed who you are and your God given power to succeed in this world, you are bound to make it in this life no matter all the odds that may be against you. Start today and pursue the things that belong to you. Yes you can, for you are not alone. You have all the resources, the talent, and God given power to succeed. Yes, your resources need to grow and continue to multiply. When all the principles are taken into consideration and put to work effectively, then success is bound to come. You are the one who will change the situation around you and not anyone else. Your destiny is in your own hands. God will never override your will or change the situation around you without your concern. He is a God of principles and never a usurper of authority. God has all power and authority but never abuses it as we do. When we yield our will to Him, He will then work with us to bring the best in us. He has made us to succeed, and no one take that from us but ourselves.

The following principles will help us not only to succeed but also grow and increase our resources.

1. Believe it is God's will to prosper you

Many people find it difficult to realize what God has in store for them and the world as a whole. The Scriptures makes it clear that for lack of knowledge my people are destroyed. Your situation will never change whether you know or you don't. It is one thing not to know, but it is another knowing and not doing it. We have to come to the realization that God has given us all things that pertain to life and godliness. God has created in the world the abundance of everything that man needs and there is enough for all. We need to make use of what God has given us.

There are so many natural resources on earth for all to enjoy. The only thing you and I have to do is to know that they belong to us. We therefore have to tap into them. Some people think it is not God's will to prosper and be successful. They despise riches, thinking it is a sin to be rich. Remember, money is not evil when it is honestly gained and honestly used. If it is not the will of God to prosper why did he place all the resources on the earth? You need to take your share of the resources. They will not fall into your lap if you don't take them. Grab your God given share and run with it. But don't let it get into your head. The money is given to you so that you can also give in turn. I personally think that life in abundance also includes prosperity. Make use of your God given power and authority. Enjoy what has been given to you. Don't allow anyone to deprive you of your God given right. Your destiny is in your hands. Make the most of it. You success and your prosperity will always be determined by your knowledge of your rights.

We sometimes have the audacity to blame others for the lack of success. Anytime you point a finger at others for the lack of success you need to remember that four of the other fingers are pointing back at you. It is unacceptable to be satisfied or endure defeat if it is within one's power to do otherwise. When you change your attitude, your success will also change. Let what God has in store for you benefit you. You have been made to prosper so go ahead and work it to your advantage.

2. Make God your partner for life

One of the most important laws of prosperity or success is the realization of who God is. Since He is your Maker, it will be perfect to make Him your business partner for life. He is the one who will always have your interest at heart. Give God the centre position of your business proposals. Talk to him about your business issues. Let nothing slip without his concern. Don't make a move without making sure it is His will. Let Him run your affairs, and success is bound to come.

When we turn our Scriptures to Mathew 7: 7-11 it says:

> Ask and it will be given to you; seek, and you will find, knock, and it will be opened to you. For everyone who asks, receives, and he who seeks finds, and to him that knocks it will be opened. Or what man is there among you who, if is son asks for bread, will give him a stone? Or if he asks for fish will give him a serpent? If you then being evil know how to give good gifts to your children, how much more will your father who is in heaven give good things to those who ask him.

Our God is ever ready to give unto us the things that we need when we ask. Remember He is your partner for life. We can't just dump Him and use Him when we want. He should take the centre stage to run our affairs. God should be the CEO of your company, the commander-in-chief of your army, the general overseer of your ministry, the king of your kingdom, the PR for all your affairs, and the very head of your family. This is what will bring your success. He has the master plan of your entire life. Nothing makes God happier than to see His children or partners blessed, happy, and successful in all that they do in life.

If you are making God your partner, then you need to surrender your entire life to Him and obedience to His word. John 15: 7 says, "If you abide in me, and my words abide in you, you will ask what you desire, and it shall be done for you". Find what the word of God says concerning your situation, your business, and your health, your family and pray for them to come to pass in your life. When we know the word, then we can pray better to God to bring to pass the success that we desire.

3. Make sure you do what you have been gifted to do in this life

What have you been called to do? Is it what you are doing? What do you think your talents are? Each and everyone has a God given talent, but what do we do with it? Today, many high-profile companies are looking for talented people to work with. My question is why? It is all because no matter how well a person trains in a profession it will always be the talented person who will win. When you are talented with little training you will exceed your expectation. Talent is your God given gift, and no one takes it from you. The only person who can hinder your success in terms of your talent is yourself.

If there is a job which you have talent for, why do you do one that you are not even comfortable with? No matter how much comes in at the end of the month if you do not enjoy doing it the ultimate satisfaction will never be achieved. God will always make sure you prosper in the talent that he has given you if you put it to work. What is the point of giving your whole life into a work that you know perfectly well is not what God has for you? If it is God given, then there will be faithfulness and honesty in the delivery for the blessing of God to manifest. Make use of your gifts and the fruit of it would be joy and fulfilment.

Mathew 25: 14-28 reads:

> For the kingdom of heaven is like a man traveling to a far country, which called his own servants and delivered his goods to them. And to one he gave five talents, to another two, and to another one, to each according to his own ability; and immediately he went on a journey. Then he who has received the five talents went and traded with them, and made another five talents. And likewise he who had received two gained two more also. But he who had received one went and in the ground and hid his Lord's money. After a long time the lord of those servants came and settled account with them.

> So he who had received five talents came and brought five other talents, saying, Lord, you delivered to me five talents, look; I have gained five more talents besides them. His lord said to him well done, good and faithful servant; you were faithful over few things, I will make you ruler over many things. Enter into the joy of your

lord. He also who had received two talents came and said, Lord you delivered to me two talents, look I have gained two more talents besides them. His lord said to him, well done good and faithful servant; you have been faithful over few things, I will make you a ruler over many things. Enter into the joy of your lord.

Then he who had received the one talent came and said, Lord I know you are a hard man, reaping where you have not sown, and gathering where you have not scattered seed. And I was afraid, and went and hid your talent in the ground. Look, there you have what is yours. But his lord answered and said to him, you wicked and lazy servant, you know that I reap where I have not sown, and gather where I have not scattered seed. So you ought to have deposited my money with the bankers, and at my coming I would have received back my own with interest. So take the talent from him, and give it to him who has ten talents.

Like these servant in this story we can choose to do whatever we want with our talent or gifts but the blessing or the consequences will be ours. We will all have to give account one way or the other. Those who work very hard always reap the benefit. Do remember that to him that has, more will be given. If we laze about with our God given gift, even what we have will be taken away. Our God given dream and vision is for a purpose. So arise and work with it to accomplish that purpose.

4. Your success will be based on your faith in your God

The Scriptures make it plan that he who dwells in the secret place of the Most High shall abide under the shadow of the Almighty. The men who trust in God are those who live close to him. Why? Because he is majestic, and under his wings we find shelter where we are fully secured. If we are going to walk with God then we must trust, adhere, and obey him. We need to understand his love for us. Remember not that we love him but that he loves us even while we were yet sinners Christ died for us. God is ready to give us all things that we need in this life that our joy becomes complete.

You need to overcome opposition to your progress by having that supernatural faith in God. All your obstacles and hindrances in this life would be small and will shrink to nothing when you compare it to the promise of God in faith.

When your troubles seem like giants in every corner of your life and business, then let faith arise in you that, He that has promised is faithful and that he will bring it to pass. One thing we should remember is that unbearable situations will arise. Our giants will arise and show forth their sticky heads. They will storm around like bees with their stingers. They sometimes show up like scorpions, spiders, and vipers, ready to torment. Do remember that you are an overcomer, and the victory has been won. He that is in you is greater than he that is in the world. Even if the enemy comes in like a flood, the spirit of the Lord would raise up a standard against him. If you have entrusted your business into God's hands, then you need not fear, for He is capable enough to bring it into perfect conclusion.

Psalms 37: 5 says, "Commit your ways to the Lord, trust also in him, and he shall bring it to pass". Remember that it is not you who is bringing it to pass. It is God. Not your strength but the one who has called you by His grace and mercy. You by yourself cannot make it through even a day. But with God all things are possible.

John 15: 7 says, "If you abide in me and my words abide in you, you will ask what you desire, and it shall be done for you". Do you have the word of God? Do they abide in you? Then whatsoever you desire, when you ask it will be given to you. It is a promise with a condition. When we do our part by having faith in God's word then God will also fulfil his promise to us. Faith begins where the will of God is known. When we know the will of God for our life, then we can claim it through prayer. It will not just fall on your lap. You need to pray for it to come to pass.

1 John 5: 1-4 says:

> Whoever believes that Jesus is the Christ is born of God, and everyone who loves him who begot also loves him who is begotten of him. By this we know that we love the children of God, when we love God and keep his commandments. For this is the love of God, that we keep his commandment. And his commandments are not burdensome. For whatever is born of God overcomes the world. And this is the victory that has overcome the world, our faith.

Faith does not just sit down and wait for something to happen, it works. It does take action for what it believes. Your faith only becomes complete with works. When a situation arises, faith speaks to the positive end of the situation. Faith-filled words are like seeds that are sown. You don't need proof for faith to work. Your faith should rest in the resurrected power of Jesus, and that alone will be enough. When you sit down and say you can't, it will never ever happen. Why? It is because you have sown a negative seed, which you are bound to harvest. This faith can be tested at any time. But one thing it doesn't do is to look at the circumstances that come its way. It keeps pressing on until the end is good. Your faith is the vehicle that will transport you to the destination of success.

5. Do not allow fear to hinder you from pursuing new opportunities that come your way

Fear has been one of the key issues that, if not dealt with, will destroy and shut the windows of opportunity. We need to realize that the God, who helps us with little, is equally capable to help us in bigger situations. Fear has destroyed many believers' dreams and visions. One thing that we tend to forget is that we are in covenant with God, and that he is ready to fulfil his part in the covenant promises. Our part is to have no fear but trust that he will do it. Learn to hold on to the opportunities that come your way. God is able to open more doors to you if you do not fear. Believe in yourself and in your God. Don't let limitations hinder you in your progress. Treat them as a guide to your success and a measuring rod to your victory.

Always remember to let God lead you in your new ventures, as to how far you should go, how much to invest, and for how long you should borrow. Do not allow your debts to dictate how your life and business should be run. This is all the more reason why you don't have to go into debt beyond your ability to pay back. When you borrow you should pay but also on time. Remember, your profit buys the luxuries and not your capital.

Don't rush for riches for they lead to fear—fear of failure, fear of closure, fear of imprisonment, fear of disappointment. Yes, they will come and intimidate you in your miscalculations. But if you will watch your finance and plan accordingly, these fears will not arise. Always let common sense dictate to you. You can always grow if you stay within your ability and take care of the business. Always remember to build on a solid foundation that will last forever.

6. Seek the Kingdom and its righteousness

The Scriptures always admonish believers to seek the Kingdom first, not riches. All the riches on earth belong to us, but that doesn't mean we should be chasing for riches.

Luke 12: 15 says, "And he said to them, Take heed and beware of covetousness, for one's life does not consist in the abundance of things he possesses". We have all things that we need in this life so there is no need to be covetous. Paul says godliness with contentment is great gain. We should major in important issues and minor in things less important. We need to seek the Kingdom blessing and not earthly things. The things that we see are temporary, but the ones we do not see are eternal.

Mathew 10: 37 says, "He who loves father or mother more than me is not worthy of me. And he who loves son or daughter more than me is not worthy of me". Those who will be glorified with Christ in his Kingdom are those who suffer with him. Believers need to follow the Kingdom principles to obtain the Kingdom blessing. Are you in the Kingdom? Then the blessings of the Kingdom belong to you. Forget it if you don't belong to the Kingdom. The blessing of the father belongs to the sons and the servants but not outsiders. Make up your mind as to where you belong. For if you are neither cold or hot the Scripture says he will vomit you out of his mouth.

7. Remember and obey the rule of love in your dealings

Love is the key principle of all the things we do in this life. If your life is not led in love then you have a problem. You do unto others what you want them to do unto you, nothing more nothing less. When this golden principle is over looked, then disaster will strike. Never take advantage of anyone to prosper in this life. Give the service required and the promise given for the value of money that is received. Never sell to the public goods and services that you will not use yourself. If it is not good for you, then don't bring it to the public. Don't be selfish or dishonest. Always be truthful, real, and attractive to all no matter your age, appearance, education, colour, or position in life.

Power and radiance come from a change of heart and also from Christ living inside of you. Good qualities come from the inside, not from the outward appearance. We are loved, and even while we were yet sinners Christ died for us, the ungodly. When you give love, it will be returned back to you. So also when you sow hate you will reap hate. You can through foul means make it in life but remember the end awaits you. Remember every seed sown would be reaped, and the increase would always be there.

1 John4: 7-11 says:

> Beloved, let us love one another, for love is of
> God; and everyone who loves is born of God
> and know GOD, for God is love. In this the love
> of God was manifested toward us, that God has
> sent his only begotten Son into the world, that we
> might live through Him. In this is love, not that
> we loved God, but that he loved us and sent His
> Son to be the propitiation for our sins. Beloved,
> if God so loved us, we also ought to love one
> another.

No one can put it simpler than John has done here. We are
given so we should give. We are loved so in return we should
love. If we are living through Christ, and he is loved, then we
need to love. The nature of God in us is love. You therefore
need to exhibit it in all your life and dealings.

Romans 12: 9-21 reads:

> Let love be without hypocrisy. Abhor what
> is evil. Cling to what is good. Be kindly
> affectionate to one another with brotherly love,
> in honour giving preference to one another; not
> lagging in diligence, fervent in spirit, serving the
> Lord; rejoicing in hope, patient in tribulation,
> continuing steadfastly in prayer, distributing
> to the needs of the saints, giving to hospitality.
> Bless those who persecute you; bless and do not
> curse. Rejoice with those who rejoice, weep with
> those who weep. Be of the same mind toward one
> another. Do not set your mind on high things, but
> associate with the humble. Do not be wise in your

own opinion. Repay no one evil for evil. Have regard for good things in the sight of all men. If it is possible as much as depends on you, live peaceably with all men. Beloved do not avenge yourselves, but rather give place to wrath; for it is written, vengeance is mine, I will repay, says the Lord. Therefore, if your enemy is hungry, feed him, if he is thirsty, give him to drink, for in so doing you will heap coals of fire on his head. Do not be overcome by evil, but overcome evil with good.

We should always remember that God is love and that he has no plans to tempt us to punish us. Peace is not something that we have control of, but we can love. Do not seek personal revenge—let God do the punishing. We always feed and give drink to our enemies so they can realize their faults and repent from them. Coals of fire make them realize their shame and repent and then experience purification as a result. When our enemies repent, we can be at peace with them, and that is the joy of it. An enemy can become a friend. This is the phenomenal power of God's love that believers are connected to through Christ our Lord.

1 Thessalonians 4: 9-12 reads:

But concerning brotherly love you have no need that I should write to you, for you yourselves are taught by God to love one another, and indeed you do so toward all the brethren who are in Macedonia. But we urge you brethren, that you increase more and more that you aspire to lead a quiet life, to mind your own business, and to work with your own hands, as we commanded

you, that you may walk properly toward those
who are outside, and that you may lack nothing.

Paul here admonished the church not only to love but also
to increase in love. A quiet life is befitting to the Christian
faith. Instead of becoming busybodies we need to mind our
own business. We need to run our own affairs and not be busy
running the affairs of others. Believers must learn to focus on
our own business for the success that we seek.

If you start with giving rather than getting, you will never suffer
lack and succeed in life. People can stop you from receiving
money but they cannot stop you from giving money. It is your
giving that brings you blessing not receiving. Give your good
will, your wishes, your time, your talents, your life, and your
all, and you will be receiving from both God and men you
blessed. When you give your supply will never be exhausted.

Philippians 4: 13 says, "I can do all things through Christ who
strengthen me".

Believers' true sufficiency is found in Christ. If you have
Christ, then you can do because Christ can. Success comes to
those who can. It is God who makes us able to abound. If you
are crucified with Christ, then as Paul said you no longer live
but Christ lives. If Christ can, then you can, because your life
is rooted and grounded in Christ. I can, because Christ can and
therefore success is mine.

Conclusion

You may have just finished reading this book and may be wondering where to start and when to start. You are likely to say to yourself, *But I don't have the means.* You may be more confused than ever, not knowing what to do. The answer is very simple.

1. Find your identity, which begins with knowing Christ Jesus as Lord.

2. Know that God has a plan and a purpose for you: to prosper and to give you a perfect end. It is his desire to prosper you in every area of your life and make your name great.

3. Believe that he has placed within you a gift, which when discovered and natured can be a great assert and a blessing. It is this knowledge that will lead you to places and set you before kings and nobles.

4. Begin to put to use the little that you have and let your money work for you.

5. Cut all unnecessary expenses and start paying yourself.

6. Believe in yourself that it shall be good and that you can make it.

7. Take it a day at a time and plan and execute your plans effectively.

8. Know your vision will come to pass with much business.

9. Let faith have its perfect work in you by spending time in the word of God, and prayer as your back bone.

10. Conduct your business wisely and let proper business principles serve as a guide in your daily business activities.

Remember there are many business strategies that I have introduced in this book. Take time to read them over and over again until you get used to them. Apply them in your business life where necessary. God believes in you, and so do I. Your future is bright and awesome. You will surely see your light at the end of your tunnel. God has not given you up so don't give up on yourself. He surely has a perfect plan for you. Seek those things above, and the rest would just be bonus.

When you fall, try and lift yourself up and shake off the dust and mud and move on, because you can. When you hang on, success will be guaranteed. *Remember assiduous people always make it to the finish line, and I strongly believe that you are one of them.* Yes you can!